W9-BAI-097

crochet
me

crochet me

kim werker

PHOTOGRAPHY: Jeff Navarro UNLESS OTHERWISE NOTED
COVER AND INTERIOR DESIGN: Karla Baker
ILLUSTRATIONS: Cynthia Frenette

Interweave Press LLC
201 East Fourth Street
Loveland, CO 80537-5655 USA
interweavebooks.com

Printed and bound in China through Asia Pacific Offset

Library of Congress Cataloging-in-Publication Data

Werker, Kim P.
Crochet me : designs to fuel the crochet revolution / Kim Werker, author.
p. cm.
Includes index.
ISBN-13: 978-1-59668-044-9 (pbk.)
1. Crocheting--Patterns. I. Title.
TT820.W373 2007
746.43'4041--dc22

2007015111

10 9 8 7 6 5 4 3 2 1

ACKNOWLEDGMENTS

The designers featured here dove into the depths of their creativity to make the patterns you're about to enjoy, and I had the pleasure and honor of working with them on this project. Their friendship and inspiration are more special to me than I can say.

Tricia Waddell told me something any writer dreams of hearing from her editor: "Don't hold back." Her valued support, guidance, and partnership resulted in the greatest creative experience I've ever had. Thanks also to Linda Stark, Rebecca Campbell, and Marilyn Murphy, who were as much a part of this wild ride. Finally, to Jaime Guthals, Laura Levaas, and Annie Bakken, for the excitement that's to come.

In addition to designing two projects for the book, Julie Holetz technical edited the whole shebang. Given that that we went out of our way to break out of normal approaches to crochet, I certainly handed her a doozy of a manuscript, and she thoughtfully attended to it.

To the Fiber League, crafty friends and colleagues, thank you for the constant stream of ideas and support. Hugs to my bff, Emma Jane Hogbin, for taking CrochetMe.com to the next level with me, and for making it such fun along the way.

To friends near and far who are as much family as fun-makers, high fives all around. Thanks to the Werkers, Feldmans, and Geffens for making me a part of the family from the get-go, and for sharing your excitement and support for this crazy crochet adventure.

Mentions of my parents and grandparents grace many pages of this book, just as they have infused my life with love, support, creativity, and laughter. I love them as much as you might think, and likely more. I also love my brother, who isn't really into the yarn stuff, and so doesn't play as large a part in this book as he plays in my life. Finally, my gratitude and love to Greg.

To Greg:
Maker of laughs,
giver of hugs,
keeper of what's
said around the
kitchen table.

contents

an open letter 8

BABYDOLL DRESS 10
by Amy O'Neill Houck
Designer in Profile: Amy O'Neill Houck 15

ICELANDIC TURTLENECK 16
by Chloe Nightingale
Technically Speaking: Crochet Stitching 24
Designer in Profile: Chloe Nightingale 25

VICTORIAN SHRUG + WRAP 26
by Robyn Chachula
Technically Speaking: Reading Stitch Diagrams 34
Designer in Profile: Robyn Chachula 35

MINI WRAP SKIRT 36
by Amy O'Neill Houck
Essay: A Different Kind of Post 41

MESSENGER BAG 42
by Julie Armstrong Holetz
Designer in Profile: Julie Armstrong Holetz 47

I'M A CONVERT SWEATER 48
by Melissa Hills
Technically Speaking: A Note on Gauge 54
Designer in Profile: Melissa "Missa" Hills 55

STYLE MODERNE JEWELRY 56
by Chloe Nightingale

MESMERIZE SWEATER 60
by Kristin Omdahl
Technically Speaking: Block It! Just Block It! 66
Designer in Profile: Kristin Omdahl 67

SHADES OF PLAID SCARVES 68
by Julie Armstrong Holetz
Technically Speaking: Crochet Sampler 71

LEAVES SWEATER 72
by Annette Petavy
Designer in Profile: Annette Petavy 82
Essay: Generations 83

THIGH HIGHS 84
by Cecily Keim
Designer in Profile: Cecily Keim 89

COMFY CARDI 90
by Robyn Chachula
Technically Speaking: Shaping 97

FIVE O'CLOCK TANK 98
by Megan Granholm
Designer in Profile: Megan Granholm 111
Technically Speaking: Tunisian Crochet 112

COCOON BAG 114
by Cecily Keim

VARIATIONS BASKETS 118
by Carol Ventura
Technically Speaking: Tapestry Crochet 122
Designer in Profile: Carol Ventura 123

CIRCLE RUG 124
by Donna Hulka
Technically Speaking: The Adjustable Ring 130
Designer in Profile: Donna Hulka 131

DOUG + GORDO DOLLS 132
by Kim Werker

postscript 137
abbreviations 138
glossary 139
resources 142
index 143

an *open letter*

PHOTO BY PAMELA BETHEL

One word, dear crocheters:

EMPOWERMENT.

That's the thing that motivates me most: It's what drove me to start CrochetMe.com, the website that inspired this book, and it's what then drove me to write this book.

Cue the cheesy TV harp music and join me on a bit of a memory bender . . .

Picture this: One Saturday during the winter of 2004, I was sitting in my basement office surfing the 'Net. I was desperately seeking crochet patterns. I wanted to make pretty stuff. Stuff with attitude that reflected my attitude. I wanted cool crochet. What I found, though, were 1996-era purple, blinking sites with better photos of people's cats than the crochet projects they claimed to be showing off. I searched harder and looked deeper. Finally, in a fit of frustration and boredom (do you know how dark it can be during a winter afternoon in Vancouver?), I set up a subdomain on my freelance Web design business site and CrochetMe.com was born. I had barely finished my first crochet project in several years, so I wasn't prepared to churn out wicked patterns to share. I confess I was as motivated to make a nonblinking, nonpurple, noncluttered, non-pet-riddled crochet site as I was to find cool crochet patterns to publish. I posted about the new site on a few message boards, shut down my computer for the day, and went about my weekend business.

Within two weeks I was getting e-mail from women in the United States, Europe, and Australia. I started receiving patterns, articles, and tutorials to publish. It was way fun. Months passed. Then it got to be time-consuming and in fact a bit all-consuming, and I found myself in an all-or-nothing situation. I consulted with my partner. I lamented having managed by age 27 to be a twice grad school drop-out, an adult summer camp counselor, an overworked underpaid community center employee with stress-induced stomach aches, a substitute teacher, and a mediocre-at-best freelance web designer. We figured, *why not*?

So I made CrochetMe.com an online magazine. Annette Petavy (one of the first crocheters to contact me when I started the site) agreed to write for it regularly. Some months later, Julie Holetz took on technical editing, later to be helped out by Chloe Nightingale and Jenna Nelson.

All the while, new and returning designers submitted designs for publication. All were interested in pushing crochet's boundaries. Some had never designed anything before the project they submitted. Some had been designing for years but had never considered having their patterns published; others were intimidated by the formality of print magazine submission requirements and found less stress in submitting to an informal website. With one exception, all were women.

A community developed. Contributing designers and writers brainstormed ideas for themes, for site improvements, for ways to push crochet further and to reach a wider audience. We started to find opportunities to meet each other face to face. I started to get paid work in the crochet industry, as did many other Crochet Me-ites. It was like living a dot-com dream while also making friends and being crafty, although without a billion dollars.

Eventually, I started to feel like a fairly competent editor. I started talking more with designers about their designs, the yarns they chose, and the colors they featured. Then in a profound and fortunate turn of events, I became the editor of a print magazine—*Interweave Crochet*. It was all that I wanted to be when I grew up.

So CrochetMe.com isn't an online magazine anymore. The back issues are still live, and they're still worth several hours' perusal. But now the active site is an interactive community that continues to push the boundaries of crochet, just without print-style editorial oversight. It's a crocheter's playground, overwhelming enthusiasts with free patterns and offering new and experienced designers a forum for their work. Go have a look. We'll welcome you warmly.

So, back to empowerment. From the day I first started CrochetMe.com, I've learned some things about people. Lots of people are intimidated by creativity; they're afraid to try new things and fail. I propose that fear simply isn't an appropriate term to apply to crochet. Crochet doesn't involve breakable things, for the most part. Nothing to lacerate, bruise, bludgeon, burn, or otherwise cause illness, suffering, or the loss of livelihood. In other words, there's simply nothing to fear. Sure, we all feel vulnerable when we create something. *What if I think it's gorgeous but everyone else thinks it's hideous? What if I have an image in my head but my hands can't make it? What if it doesn't fit? What if the recipient hates it and only smiles to be polite?* All uncomfortable scenarios, for sure. But no reason to feel fear. No reason not to try.

It's astonishing the number of times someone has told me she had never considered that she could use a different color to crochet a particular pattern, or she could alter a pattern to make it fit her body more flatteringly. *Astonishing.* This, dear readers, is not okay. If we don't allow ourselves—force ourselves, sometimes—to think creatively, to behave creatively, to take creative risks, how are we to discover our own potential?

It's empowering to trust ourselves. To explore ourselves. To express ourselves. That's what this book is all about. Beyond telling the stories of women who have done all those things, it's a 144-page plea to you, personally. Try something new. Experiment. Don't back down. Value your work and your time. When you're done, learn to love it even if you hate it. Learn from it, period. Sit back, take a deep breath, and assess the damage and the benefits. Smile. Repeat. Post lots of photos.

ABOUT THIS BOOK

Two goals were always in my mind as I worked on this book. The first was to compile an assortment of designs that show off crochet at its best and present techniques to interest crocheters of all sorts. The second was to kick you in the pants to explore your creativity, to arm you with the tools to enable you to do so in crochet specifically, and to introduce you to some of the women who have inspired me in all of those ways over the years.

Throughout the book, you'll find *designer profiles* that introduce you to a rich and diverse crochet community. I asked the designers featured here a standard list of questions, and their answers consistently fascinated me. Each pattern also has an introduction in the designer's own words, offering insight into her creative process and the inspiration behind the design. Also look for the *technically speaking* sidebars that present crochet techniques plus *essays* about how crochet has empowered and inspired me. If you see an abbreviation or term you don't recognize, check the Glossary on page 138.

Every project has a *concentration rating*, so you know how much focus is required to successfully complete it:

1 Crochet it at a party. Very little direct concentration needed. You'll be able to chat the night away.

2 Crochet it in front of the TV. The stitch pattern is easy to memorize so after a little bit you'll be on autopilot.

3 Crochet it with mood music. You'll probably want to watch your work progress, but you'll have enough spare energy to occasionally hum along.

4 Defcon 5! Crochet it in a quiet room. Turn the telephone off—you'll want your full attention on your work. When it's finished, bragging rights will be yours.

Remember, this book is intended to be a jumping-off point. Google anything you see mentioned in this book to learn more about it. Join CrochetMe.com and ask questions, share tips, post patterns, and meet people. I don't know you, but I've had you in mind for years. Come say hello.

Cheers,

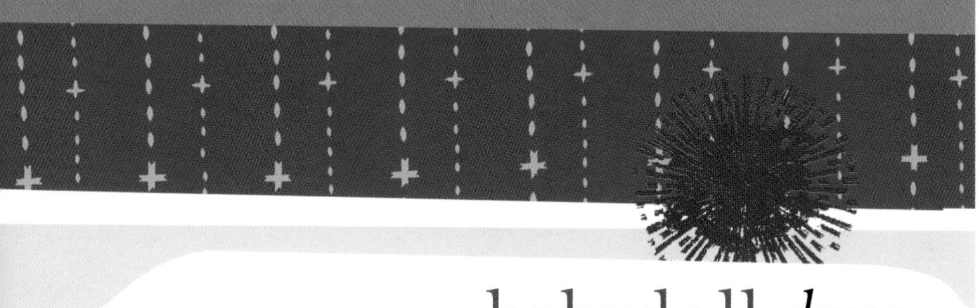

babydoll *dress*

Amy O'Neill Houck

concentration rating 1 2 3 4

AMY'S INSPIRATION

When designing this dress, I was inspired by the great layered fashions I was seeing in magazines and stores—little dresses worn over jeans and long T-shirts that mixed lacy and casual. A sleeveless tunic worked in thread crochet that I found at a thrift store inspired the stitch patterns I used in the lace of this modular crochet babydoll dress.

FINISHED SIZE

BUST CIRCUMFERENCE: 32 (34, 36, 38, 40)" (81.5 [86.5, 91.5, 96.5, 101.5] cm) to fit bust sizes 30 (32, 34, 36, 38)" (76 [81.5, 86.5, 91.5, 96.5] cm). The dress is designed with negative ease in the bodice ribbing, so if you want a looser fit, make a size larger.

YARN

Brown Sheep Cotton Fleece (80% cotton/20% merino wool; 215 yd [197 m]/3.5 oz): # CW-105 Putty, 6 (6, 7, 7, 8) skeins.

SUBSTITUTION: About 1,127 (1,200, 1,277, 1,352, 1,428) yd (1,031 [1,097, 1,168, 1,236, 1,306] m) DK weight (Light #3) yarn.

HOOK

Sizes G/6 (4 mm), H/8 (5 mm), and I/9 (5.5 mm). Change hook size if necessary to obtain the correct gauge.

NOTIONS

Lace ribbon, 1" (2.5 cm) wide, 2 (2¼, 2¼, 2½, 2½)" (5 [5.5, 5.5, 6.5, 6.5] cm) long, yarn needle.

GAUGE

Ribbing: 20 sc-blo and 19 rows = 4" (10 cm).

Skirt: For gauge swatch use Shells and Chains Skirt Pattern on page 12. Repeat pattern Rows 2 and 3 until swatch measures 5" (13 cm) wide and 6" (15 cm) long.

+ SPECIAL STITCHES +

SC-BLO: Work sc through back loop only.

SHALLOW SINGLE CROCHET (SSC): Insert hook into the center of the single crochet stitch, between the 2 vertical threads, instead of just below the 2 top loops. This forms a stacked "V" look for the strip of single crochet stitches.

SHELL (SH): Work 5 dc all in same stitch.

SHELLS AND CHAINS GAUGE PATTERN
(Multiple of 6 sts)

With middle-size hook, ch 22.

ROW 1: Sk first 3 chs from hook (counts as dc), 2 dc in next ch, *sk 2 ch, sc in next ch, sk 2 ch, sh in next ch; rep from * across, ending with 3 dc in last ch, turn—2 complete shells plus 2 half shells on each end.

ROW 2: Ch 1, sc in first dc, *ch 2, ssc in next sc, ch 2, sc in 3rd dc of next sh; rep from * across to end, turn.

ROW 3: Ch 3 (counts as dc), 2 dc in first dc, *ssc in next sc, sh in next sc; rep from * across to end, ending with 3 dc in last sc, turn.

+ PATTERN NOTES +

- Bodice ribbing is worked in single crochet through the back loop only (sc-blo).
- There is a subtle difference in the stitch used in the sleeves and in the skirt. In the skirt, the shells are stacked to give a distinctive vertical stripe, but in the sleeves they're staggered for a lacier look.
- The bodice is made in two identical sections, each made of five panels. The sections are then crocheted together at the back, front and underarms before the sleeves and skirt are added. The chains in the bodice are always made with the middle-size (H/8 [5 mm]) hook so the garment has adequate vertical stretch.

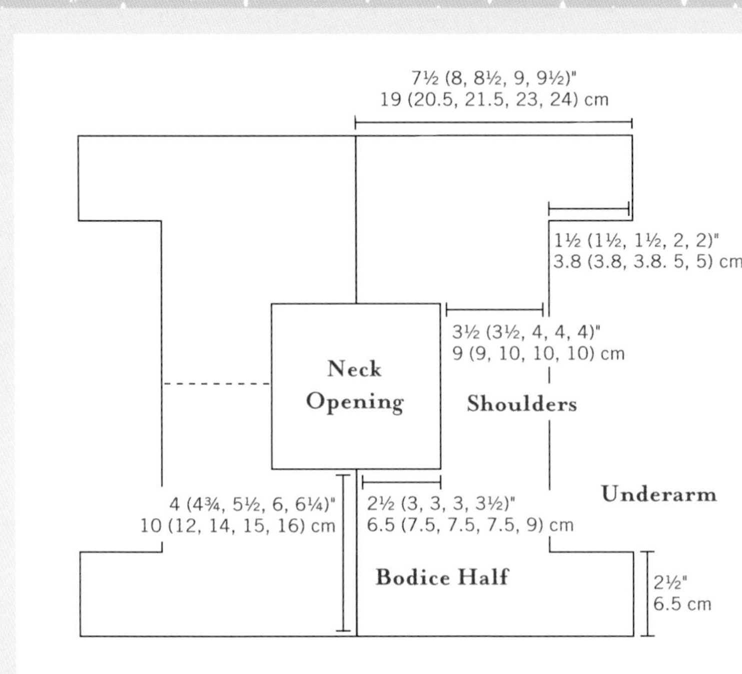

- The fit of this dress is customizable—you can adjust the length, the sleeves, and more to your liking. You could even leave the sleeves off for a cute jumper.

DRESS

BODICE HALF

(Make 2)

For a custom fit, make any of the panels wider or narrower by adding or removing rows.

FRONT PANEL

Using middle-size hook, loosely ch 22 (25, 28, 31, 32).

ROW 1: Using smallest hook, sc in second ch and in each ch across, turn—21 (24, 27, 30, 31) sts.

ROW 2: Ch 1, sc-blo (see Special Stitches) in each st across, turn.

Rep Row 2 until your work measures 2½ (3, 3, 3, 3½)" (6.5 [7.5, 7.5, 7.5, 9] cm).

SHOULDER PANEL

At the end of the next row, switch back to middle-size hook and loosely ch 69 (72, 75, 78, 79).

ROW 1: Using smallest hook, sc in ch and in each ch and sc across, turn—89 (95, 101, 107, 110) sts.

ROW 2: Ch 1, sc-blo in each st across, turn.

Rep Row 2 until shoulder panel measures 3½ (3½, 4, 4, 4)" (9 [9, 10, 10, 10] cm) across and 6 (6½, 7, 7, 7½)" (15 [16.5, 18, 18, 19] cm) from beg of Front Panel. Fasten off.

BACK PANEL

With smallest hook, join yarn to the bottom edge of the shoulder panel (opposite the front panel). Crocheting into the back loop of the foundation chain, ch 1, sc-blo in each of next 33 (36, 39, 42, 43) chs, turn.

ROW 1: Ch 1, sc-blo in each st across—33 (36, 39, 42, 43) sts.

Repeat Row 1 until back panel measures 2½ (3, 3, 3, 3½)" (6.5 [7.5, 7.5, 7.5, 9] cm). Fasten off.

UNDERARM PANEL

Rotate work 180°, with smallest hook, join yarn to the opposite open side of the shoulder panel from where you worked the back panel, ch 1, sc-blo in each of next 12 sts, turn.

ROW 1: Ch 1, sc-blo in each st across the row—12 sts.

Rep Row 1 until underarm panel measures 1½ (1½, 1½, 2, 2)" (3.8 [3.8, 3.8, 5.5, 5.5] cm). Fasten off.

Repeat underarm panel on the other end of the shoulder panel opposite from the front panel. You should have one I-shaped piece.

ASSEMBLE BODICE

You should have two I-shaped pieces. With right sides together and working through the outside loops, single crochet back seam, single crochet front seam, single crochet underarm seam.

SKIRT

The Skirt is worked down from the bodice in the round and the rounds are joined with a sl st. Do not turn work at the end of the round.

SET UP ROUND

With middle-size hook, join yarn at center back seam of bodice, ch 1, work 1 sc in the row edge of every other row, working only in the "valleys" of the ribbing. Sl st in first sc to join.

EYELET ROUND

Ch 4 (counts as dc, ch 1), *sk next st, dc in next st, ch 1; rep from * around, sl st in 3rd ch of beg ch-4 to join.

LACE

RND 1: Ch 3 (counts as dc), work 4 dc in first st, *sk next 2 sts, sc in next st, sk 2 sts, sh (see Special Stitches) in next st; rep from * around, ending with sc in last st, sl st in 3rd ch of beg ch-3 to join.

Note: If the number of sts in your skirt is not a multiple of 6, work a partial shell at the end of the

round. For a partial shell, work 3 dc in second to last st, ending with sc in last st.

RND 2: Sl st in each of next 2 dc, ch 1, sc in same st, ch 2, ssc (see Special Stitches) in next sc, ch 2, *sc in 3rd dc of next shell, ch 2, ssc in next sc, ch 2; rep from * around, sl st in first sc to join.

RND 3: Ch 3 (counts as dc), work 4 dc in first st, ssc in next sc, *sh in next sc, ssc in next sc; rep from * around, sl st in 3rd ch of beg ch-3 to join.

Rep Rnds 2 and 3 until the dress falls to your hip bone when you try it on. Change to largest hook, continue in est pattern until skirt falls just above your knee or to your desired length. End with Row 3.

Fasten off.

SLEEVES

Sleeves are worked in a similar fashion to the Skirt. All sizes are worked in the same manner because the armhole sizing was created when you crocheted the bodice.

SET UP ROUND

With middle-size hook, join yarn at underarm seam. Sc around armhole opening, working 1 sc in the edge of every other row (in the valleys) of the underarm panel, work 2 sts at each corner between underarm and shoulder panel, and 1 sc in each st around shoulder panel, sl st in first sc to join.

RND 1: Ch 3 (counts as dc), 4 dc in same st, *sk 2 sts, ssc in next sc, sk 2 sts, sh in next sc; rep from * around, ending with sc in last st, sl st in 3rd ch of beg ch-3 to join.

Note: If the number of sts in the armhole opening is not a multiple of 6, work a partial shell at the end of the round. For a partial shell, work 3 dc in second to last st, ending with sc in last st.

RND 2: Sl st in each of next 2 dc, ch 1, sc in same st, ch 2, ssc in next sc, ch 2, *sc in 3rd dc of next shell, ch 2, ssc in next sc, ch 2; rep from * around, sl st in first sc.

RND 3: Ch 1, sc in first st, *sh in next sc (bet shells), ssc in next sc (over shells); rep from * around, ending with sh in last sc, sl st in first sc to join.

RND 4: Ch 1, ssc in same st, ch 2, sc in 3rd dc of next shell, *ch 2, ssc in next sc, ch 2, sc in 3rd dc of next shell; rep from * around, sl st in first sc to join.

Rep Rnds 1–4 twice (add a repeat for a slightly longer sleeve). Work Rnds 1–3 once more.

SHAPE SLEEVE

RND 1: Ch 1, sc2tog around sleeve, sl st in first sc to join.

RND 2: Ch 1, sc in each st around sleeve, sl st in first sc to join.

SLEEVE RIBBING

Sleeve ribbing is worked sideways and joined as you go with 2 sl sts.

Switch to smallest hook, ch 4.

ROW 1: Sc in 2nd ch from hook and in each ch across, join ribbing to sleeve with sl st just below row of sc just worked, sl st in next sleeve st (acts as turning ch), turn—3 sc.

ROW 2: Sc-blo in each st across, turn.

ROW 3: Ch 1, sc-blo in each st across, join ribbing to sleeve with sl st, sl st in next sleeve st, turn.

Repeat Rows 2 and 3 until you've worked ribbing all the way around the sleeve opening. Sew ribbing edges together. Fasten off.

FINISHING

Weave in ends. Wash gently by hand, roll in towel to remove excess water, then block flat (see Block It sidebar on page 66). Weave ribbon through eyelet round and tie.

designer in profile

amy o'neill houck

PHOTO BY JAMES P. HOUCK

The vowel sound in Amy's last name is the same as in *ouch*. Just in case you were wondering. I wondered until I met her in person and asked. I figured I'd save you the awkward question.

Amy is a crochet and knitting designer and teacher, a writer, a technical editor, and a mom of two of the cutest kids I've ever met. She grew up a faculty brat in a college town in upstate New York.

She loves yarns of all sorts and rarely blames the yarn for producing an undesirable fabric. This is a common idea expressed by many passionate crochet designers—producing a lovely product takes thought and skill; to say crochet is ugly is not only to throw the baby out with the bathwater, it's also to tacitly admit you haven't tried very hard.

Amy approaches all aspects of crochet in terms of a greater context, be it design, education, environmentalism, or consumerism. As she puts it, "I think crochet can be a vehicle for change in all sorts of ways: educationally—because it helps young minds with math, concentration, fine motor skills; environmentally since I think about my yarn purchases the same way I think about all my purchases and always ask who made this and how does its manufacture affect the earth and those involved in its production; and politically because I love working with yarn companies who make social entrepreneurship a big part of their mission by using organic raw materials, working with cooperative spinners, dyers, artisans, and supporting the communities where they get their yarn."

A secondary skill Amy has developed is that of removing chocolate stains from fabrics of all sorts. A big, big fan of dark chocolate, specifically, she jokes (I think) that if you look closely, you might find a mark of chocolate on the dress she designed on page 10. Having tried desperately myself to remove a chocolate stain from a belt I crocheted for a book once, this makes me smile. We all do it. Admit it.

Amy started calling herself a designer after her first design was published. "I'm not too shy about titles," she says. "I think if you want to be something, you should start thinking of yourself with that title; it helps you reach that goal."

AMY WRITES A BLOG AT HOOKANDI.BLOGSPOT.COM AND HAS A PROFESSIONAL SITE AT AOHDESIGNS.COM.

icelandic *turtleneck*

Chloe Nightingale

concentration rating 1 **2** 3 4

CHLOE'S INSPIRATION

Crochet sweaters get a bad rap, and I can see why. They tend to either be thick, bulky, stiff, and square, or so lacy that they don't look like they would be warm. Part of the problem is a sweater crocheted with worsted-weight or Aran-weight yarn is much thicker than a sweater knitted with the same yarn. The solution is to crochet with a thinner yarn. I picked Rowan 4-ply because it's soft and warm without being too heavy. I wanted this sweater to have good stretch to it, so I used double crochet through the back loop only to achieve this. The result is a nice, stretchy, snuggly sweater with great drape. As a variation, make an oversize, extra-long version to wear with leggings.

FINISHED SIZE

BUST CIRCUMFERENCE: 32 (35, 38, 41, 44)" (81.5 [89, 96.5, 104, 112] cm). Sweater is designed to be close-fitting.

YARN

Rowan 4-ply Soft (100% merino wool; 191 yds [175 m]/1.75 oz): #383 Black, 7 (8, 9, 10, 11) skeins. Sweater alone uses 6 (6, 7, 7, 8) skeins. Yarn distributed by Westminster Fibers.

SUBSTITUTION: About 1,225 (1,400, 1,575, 1,750, 1,925) yd (1,120 [1,280, 1,440, 1,600, 1,760] m) of sock/fingering-weight (Super Fine #1) wool yarn.

HOOK

Size D/3 (3.25 mm). Change hook size if necessary to obtain the correct gauge.

NOTIONS

Yarn needle.

GAUGE

19 dc-blo and 11 rows = 4" (10 cm).

+ SPECIAL STITCHES +

FOUNDATION DOUBLE CROCHET (FDC): Ch 3, yo, insert hook in 3rd ch from hook and pull up a lp, yo and pull through 1 lp (1 ch made), [yo and pull through 2 lps] twice (one fdc made). *Yo, insert hook under both lps of ch from previous fdc and pull up a lp, yo and pull through 1 lp (1 ch made), [yo and pull through 2 lps] twice; rep from * across. (See Glossary on page 139.)

DC-TBL: Work dc through both lps (this is the same as a dc stitch, but is used to distinguish the dc from dc-blo to avoid confusion).

FDC-TBL: This is a more secure way of joining a fdc to dc-blo. Insert hook through 1 lp on bottom post of previous fdc (counts as yo) *and* through both lps of the stitch you are working into (4 lps on hook), yo, pull lp through first 2 lps (3 lps on hook), [yo and pull through 2 lps] twice.

DC-BLO: Work dc through back loop only.

DC2TOG-BLO DECREASE: Working through back loop only, yo, insert hook in next st, draw up a lp (3 lps on hook), yo, draw through first 2 lps on hook, yo, insert hook in next st, draw up a lp (4 lps on hook), yo, draw through first 2 lps on hook, yo, draw through 3 lps on hook.

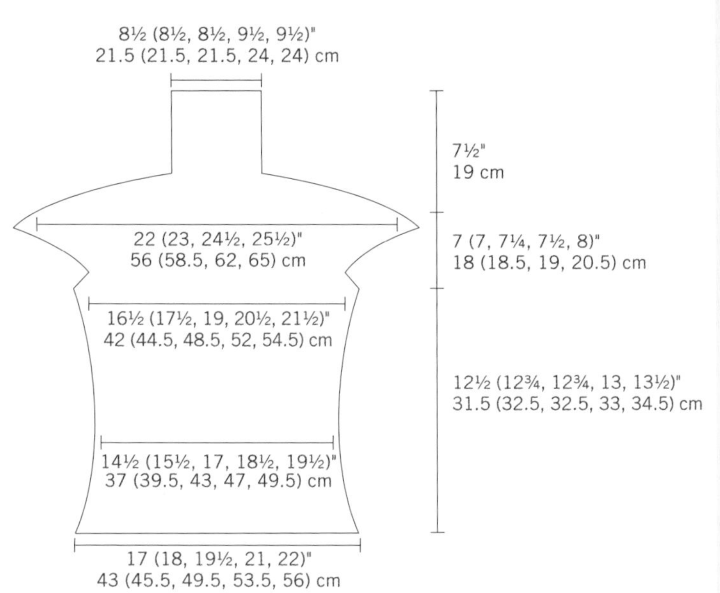

Armwarmers

8½ (8¾, 9½, 10, 11)"
21.5 (22, 24, 25.5, 28) cm

17"
43 cm

TURTLENECK

NECK

Fdc (see Special Stitches) 80 (80, 80, 90, 90), sl st in top of first Fdc to form ring, being careful not to twist chain. *Note:* There will be a small gap below the sl st (since this is a Fdc and the stitches are taller than a ch; a sl st does not sufficiently close the round at the bottom). When weaving in your ends, fasten this bit together with the tail before weaving it in.

RND 1: Ch 2 (counts as first dc here and throughout), dc-blo (see Special Stitches) in each st around, sl st in 2nd ch of beg ch-2 to join—80 (80, 80, 90, 90) sts total.

Rep Rnd 1 until piece measures 7¼" (18.5 cm) from beg of Neck.

YOKE

SIZE 32" (81.5 CM) ONLY

RND 1: Ch 2, dc-blo in next st, 2 dc-blo in next st, dc-blo in each of next 2 sts, 2 dc-blo in next st, dc-blo in each of next 3 sts, 2 dc-blo in next st, *[dc-blo in each of next 2 sts, 2 dc-blo in next st] twice, dc-blo in each of next 3 sts, 2 dc-blo in next st; rep from * around, sl st in 2nd ch of beg ch-2 to join—104 sts total.

RND 2: Ch 2, dc-blo in each st around, sl st in 2nd ch of beg ch-2 to join.

SIZE 35" (89 CM) ONLY

RND 1: Ch 2, dc-blo in next st, 2 dc-blo in next st, dc-blo in each of next 2 sts, 2 dc-blo in next st, dc-blo in next st, 2 dc-blo in next st, *[dc-blo in each of next 2 sts, 2 dc-blo in next st] twice, dc-blo in next st, 2 dc-blo in next st;,rep from * around, sl st in 2nd ch to join—110 sts total.

RND 2: Ch 2, dc-blo in each st around, sl st in 2nd ch of beg ch-2 to join.

SIZE 38" (96.5 CM) ONLY

RND 1: Ch 2, dc-blo in next st, 2 dc-blo in next st, dc-blo in each of next 2 sts, 2 dc-blo in next st, dc-blo in next st, 2 dc-blo in next st, *[dc-blo in each of next 2 sts, 2 dc-blo in next st] twice, dc-blo in next st, 2 dc-blo in next st; rep from * around, sl st in 2nd ch to join—110 sts total.

RND 2: Ch 2, dc-blo in next st, *2 dc-blo in next st, dc-blo in each of next 17 sts; rep from * around, sl st in 2nd ch to join—116 sts total.

SIZE 41" (104 CM) ONLY

RND 1: Ch 2, dc-blo in next st, 2 dc-blo in next st, *dc-blo in each of next 2 sts, 2 dc-blo in next st; rep from * around, sl st in 2nd ch to join—120 sts total.

RND 2: Ch 2, 2 dc-blo in next st, dc-blo in each of next 59 sts, 2 dc-blo in next st, dc-blo in each st to end of round, sl st in 2nd ch to join—122 sts total.

SIZE 44" (112 CM) ONLY

RND 1: Ch 2, 2 dc-blo in next st, dc-blo in each of next 2 sts, 2 dc-blo in next st, *dc-blo in next st, 2 dc-blo in next st, dc-blo in each of next 2 sts, 2 dc-blo in next st; rep from * around, sl st in 2nd ch to join—126 sts total.

RND 2: Ch 2, 2 dc-blo in next st, dc-blo in each of next 62 sts, 2 dc-blo in next st, dc-blo in each st to end of round, sl st in 2nd ch of beg ch-2 to join—128 sts total.

ALL SIZES

RND 3: Ch 2, 2 dc-blo in next st, *dc-blo in next st, 2 dc-blo in next st; rep from * around, sl st in 2nd ch of beg ch-2 to join—156 (165, 174, 183, 192) sts total.

RND 4: Ch 2, dc-blo in each st around, sl st in 2nd ch of beg ch-2 to join.

RNDS 5–7: Rep Rnd 4.

RND 8: Ch 2, dc-blo in next st, 2 dc-blo in next st, *dc-blo in each of next 2 sts, 2 dc-blo in next st; rep from * around, sl st in 2nd ch of beg ch-2 to join—208 (220, 232, 244, 256) sts total.

RND 9: Ch 2, dc-blo in each st around, sl st in 2nd ch of beg ch-2 to join.

Rep Rnd 9 for 10 (10, 11, 12, 13) more rounds. Fasten off.

BUST

RND 1: Fdc 7 (8, 9, 10, 11), Fdc-tbl (see Special Stitches) in 21st (22nd, 23rd, 24th, 25th) st from sl st seam (sl st counts as first st), dc-blo in each of next 62 (66, 70, 74, 78) sts, dc-tbl (see Special Stitches) in next st, working first Fdc through 1 lp on the bottom post of the previous dc: Fdc 14 (16, 18, 20, 22), Fdc-tbl in 41st (43rd, 45th, 47th, 49th) st from last dc-blo worked, dc-blo in each of next 62 (66, 70, 74, 78) sts, dc-tbl in next st, working first fdc through 1 lp on the bottom post of the previous dc: Fdc 7 (8, 9, 10, 11), sk next 20 (21, 22, 23, 24) sts, sl st in top of first Fdc to join round, careful not to twist—156 (168, 180, 192, 204) sts total.

RND 2: Ch 2, dc-blo in each st around, sl st in 2nd ch of beg ch-2 to join.

Rep Rnd 2 for 8 (9, 9, 10, 11) more rounds.

WAIST

RND 1: Ch 2, dc-blo in each of next 18 (19, 21, 22, 24) sts, dc2tog-blo (see Special Stitches) over next 2 sts, *dc-blo in each of next 37 (40, 43, 46, 49) sts, dc2tog-blo over next 2 sts; rep from * 2 more times, dc-blo in each st to end of round, sl st in 2nd ch of beg ch-2 to join—152 (164, 176, 188, 200) sts total.

RND 2: Ch 2, dc-blo in each st around, sl st in 2nd ch of beg ch-2 to join.

RND 3: Ch 2, dc-blo in each of next 17 (18, 20, 21, 23) sts, dc2tog-blo over next 2 sts, dc-blo in each of next 37 (40, 43, 46, 49) sts, dc2tog-blo over next 2 sts, dc-blo in each of next 35 (38, 41, 44, 47) sts, dc2tog-blo over next 2 sts, dc-blo in each of next 37 (40, 43, 46, 49) sts, dc2tog-blo over next 2 sts, dc-blo in each st to end of round, sl st in 2nd ch of beg ch-2 to join—148 (160, 172, 184, 196) sts total.

RND 4: Ch 2, dc-blo in each of next 16 (17, 19, 20, 22) sts, dc2tog-blo over next 2 sts, dc-blo in each of next 37 (40, 43, 46, 49) sts, dc2tog-blo over next 2 sts, dc-blo in each of next 33 (36, 39, 42, 45) sts, dc2tog-blo over next 2 sts, dc-blo in each of next 37 (40, 43, 46, 49) sts, dc2tog-blo over next 2 sts, dc-blo in each st to end of round, sl st in 2nd ch of beg ch-2 to join—144 (156, 168, 180, 192) sts total.

RND 5: Ch 2, dc-blo in each st around, sl st in 2nd ch of beg ch-2 to join.

RND 6: Ch 2, dc-blo in each of next 15 (16, 18, 19, 21) sts, dc2tog-blo over next 2 sts, dc-blo in each of next 37 (40, 43, 46, 49) sts, dc2tog-blo over next 2 sts, dc-blo in each of next 31 (34, 37, 40, 43) sts, dc2tog-blo over next 2 sts, dc-blo in each of next 37 (40, 43, 46, 49) sts, dc2tog-blo over next 2 sts, dc-blo in each st to end of round, sl st in 2nd ch of beg ch-2 to join—140 (152, 164, 176, 188) sts total.

RND 7: Ch 2, dc-blo in each of next 14 (15, 17, 18, 20) sts, dc2tog-blo over next 2 sts, dc-blo in each of next 37 (40, 43, 46, 49) sts, dc2tog-blo over next 2 sts, dc-blo in each of next 29 (32, 35, 38, 41) sts, dc2tog-blo over next 2 sts, dc-blo in each of next 37 (40, 43, 46, 49) sts, dc2tog-blo over next 2 sts, dc-blo in each st to end of round, sl st in 2nd ch of beg ch-2 to join—136 (148, 160, 172, 184) sts total.

RND 8: Ch 2, dc-blo in each st around, sl st in 2nd ch of beg ch-2 to join.

RNDS 9–10: Rep Rnd 8.

RND 11: Ch 2, dc-blo in each of next 14 (15, 17, 18, 20) sts, 2 dc-blo in next st, dc-blo in each of next 37 (40, 43, 46, 49) sts, 2 dc-blo in next st, dc-blo in each of next 29 (32, 35, 38, 41) sts, 2 dc-blo in next st, dc-blo in each of next 37 (40, 43, 46, 49) sts, 2 dc-blo in next st, dc-blo in each st to end of round, sl st in 2nd ch of beg ch-2 to join—140 (152, 164, 176, 188) sts total.

RND 12: Ch 2, dc-blo in each of next 15 (16, 18, 19, 21) sts, 2 dc-blo in next st, dc-blo in each of next 37 (40, 43, 46, 49) sts, 2 dc-blo in next st, dc-blo in each of next 31 (34, 37, 40, 43) sts, 2 dc-blo in next st, dc-blo in each

of next 37 (40, 43, 46, 49) sts, 2 dc-blo in next st, dc-blo in each st to end of round, sl st in 2nd ch of beg ch-2 to join—144 (156, 168, 180, 192) sts total.

RND 13: Ch 2, dc-blo in each st around, sl st in 2nd ch of beg ch-2 to join.

RND 14: Ch 2, dc-blo in each of next 16 (17, 19, 20, 22) sts, 2 dc-blo in next st, dc-blo in each of next 37 (40, 43, 46, 49) sts, 2 dc-blo in next st, dc-blo in each of next 33 (36, 39, 42, 45) sts, 2 dc-blo in next st, dc-blo in each of next 37 (40, 43, 46, 49) sts, 2 dc-blo in next st, dc-blo in each st to end of round, sl st in 2nd ch of beg ch-2 to join—148 (160, 172, 184, 196) sts total.

RND 15: Ch 2, dc-blo in each of next 17 (18, 20, 21, 23) sts, 2 dc-blo in next st, dc-blo in each of next 37 (40, 43, 46, 49) sts, 2 dc-blo in next st, dc-blo in each of next 35 (38, 41, 44, 47) sts, 2 dc-blo in next st, dc-blo in each of next 37 (40, 43, 46, 49) sts, 2 dc-blo in next st, dc-blo in each st to end of round, sl st in 2nd ch of beg ch-2 to join—152 (164, 176, 188, 200) sts total.

RND 16: Ch 2, dc-blo in each st around, sl st in 2nd ch of beg ch-2 to join.

RND 17: Ch 2, dc-blo in each of next 18 (19, 21, 22, 24) sts, 2 dc-blo in next st, *dc-blo in each of next 37 (40, 43, 46, 49) sts, 2 dc-blo in next st,* rep from * to * 2 more times, dc-blo in each st to end of round, sl st in 2nd ch of beg ch-2 to join—156 (168, 180, 192, 204) sts total.

RND 18: Ch 2, dc-blo in each of next 19 (20, 22, 23, 25) sts, 2 dc-blo in next st, dc-blo in each of next 37 (40, 43, 46, 49) sts, 2 dc-blo in next st, dc-blo in each of next 39 (42, 45, 48, 51) sts, 2 dc-blo in next st, dc-blo in each of next 37 (40, 43, 46, 49) sts, 2 dc-blo in next st, dc-blo in each st to end of round, sl st in 2nd ch of beg ch-2 to join—160 (172, 184, 196, 208) sts total.

RND 19: Ch 2, dc-blo in each st around, sl st in 2nd ch of beg ch-2 to join.

Rep Rnd 19 for 5 more rounds or until desired length.

Fasten off.

ARMWARMERS

Fdc 40 (42, 45, 48, 52) sl st in top of first Fdc to form ring, being careful not to twist chain.

RND 1: Ch 2, dc-blo in each st around, sl st in 2nd ch of beg ch-2 to join—40 (42, 45, 48, 52) sts total.

Rep Rnd 1 for 17" (43 cm) or until desired length. You might want to increase for the upper arm for a perfect fit.

Fasten off.

FINISHING

Weave in yarn ends. Gently handwash, roll in a towel to remove excess water, and block (see Block It sidebar on page 66), or simply lay flat to dry.

technically speaking: CROCHET STITCHING

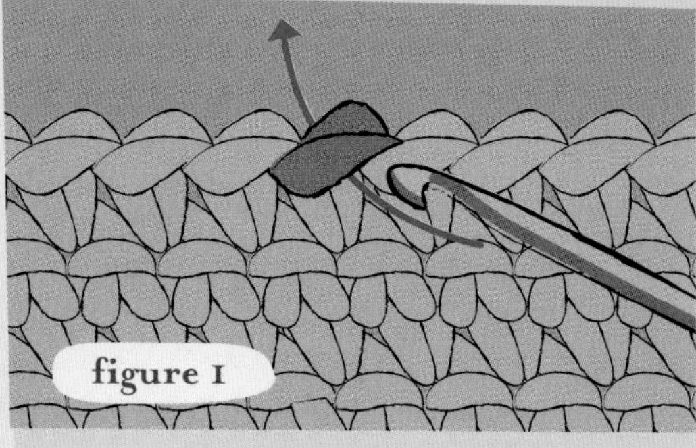
figure 1

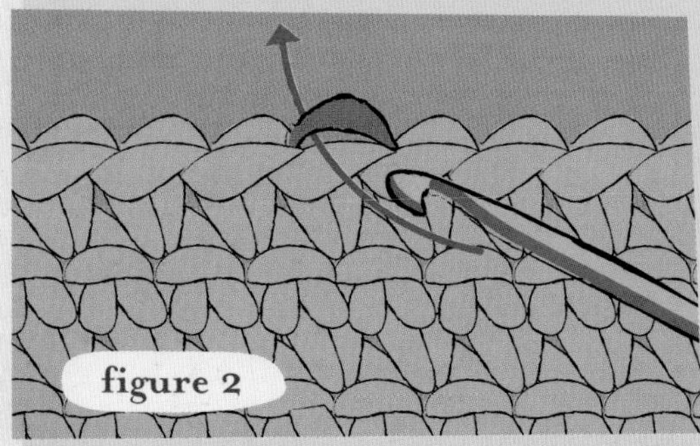
figure 2

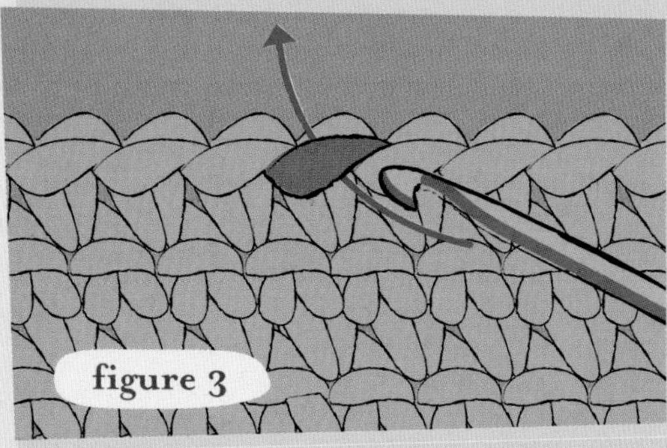
figure 3

Crochet stitching is hugely variable. The placement, height, and combination of stitches—in addition to gauge—make a big difference.

The first time I took up crochet, I was taught to stick my hook wherever I liked—because placement didn't matter. The next (and final) time I learned to crochet—the time it stuck—I learned that the loop you work your stitches into *does* matter. When no placement is specified in a pattern, it is assumed that stitches are to be worked through both loops of the stitch from the previous row (see Figure 1). This technique creates a flat, reversible fabric. When stitches are worked through the back loop only (abbreviated as *blo*, see Figure 2), a horizontal ribbed effect results. When stitches are worked through the front loop only (abbreviated as *flo*, see Figure 3), stitches become more open and drapey.

This variability is merely the tip of the iceberg, though. You can also insert your hook between stitches, around the post of a stitch from the previous row (creating stitches in relief, known as *post stitches*), or into stitches farther down than the previous row (making stitches known as *spike stitches*). You can skip stitches or make multiple stitches in the same space.

And then there's height. The basic crochet stitch is recursive in nature. To make a double crochet, you add an additional loop to the steps you take to make a single crochet. Treble crochet involves one more loop than double crochet. The only limit to how tall you can make a stitch is how many yarnovers you can fit on your hook before you insert it into the next stitch. Beyond stitch height, you can make *extended stitches*, which involves pulling the yarn through only one loop before you continue on to pull the yarn through two loops at a time. You can also work *linked stitches* or *loop stitches*. All of these are slight variations on the basics.

Finally, you can combine stitches. Bobbles, puffs, clusters, popcorns, shells, lace, mesh, filet crochet—the possibilities are endless. I highly recommend picking up a stitch dictionary and a technical tome. Here are a few I love (warning: I'm about to recommend my own book):

The Crocheter's Companion by Nancy Brown
Any of the *Harmony Guides*
The Crochet Stitch Bible by Betty Barnden
Donna Kooler's Encyclopedia of Crochet by Donna Kooler
Teach Yourself Visually Crocheting by Kim P. Werker and Cecily Keim

PHOTO BY CHANTEL KINNARD

designer in profile

chloe nightingale

Chloe is a self-proclaimed stay-at-home slacker living in Glasgow, Scotland, far, far away from the boring American suburbs where she grew up. Chloe talks a good game about her slacker ability but isn't so great with follow-through. When she started helping tech edit patterns for CrochetMe.com, she undertook a huge amount of work. Granted, she did a lot of that work in the middle of the night, so who knows what she does during the day. Lots of slacking, I guess.

Chloe prefers thinner yarns to thick ones, as you can surmise from her designs in this book. She loves finding unusual tricks and techniques in old books, and she also loves snacking on olives, though she's never crocheted one. She has, however, crocheted herself a tea bag complete with faux tag, just in case she finds herself stuck somewhere without a cup of tea.

A hooded vest made from scrap yarn was Chloe's first published pattern (CrochetMe.com, Fall 2005). It was at exactly that time that she realized most crocheters don't just wing it like she does, and she started writing patterns. She prefers crocheting with natural fibers so she can block her finished items, and cotton is her favorite. But she does value synthetics for items that will need frequent washing and for crocheted gifts when she doesn't know if the recipient might have allergies.

Chloe first launched her own website to feature her original electronic music, but she's since changed the site into Galvanic Mag, a home for her original crafts, recipes, funny stories, and cartoons, as well as music.

YOU CAN FIND CHLOE AT GALVANIC.CO.UK.

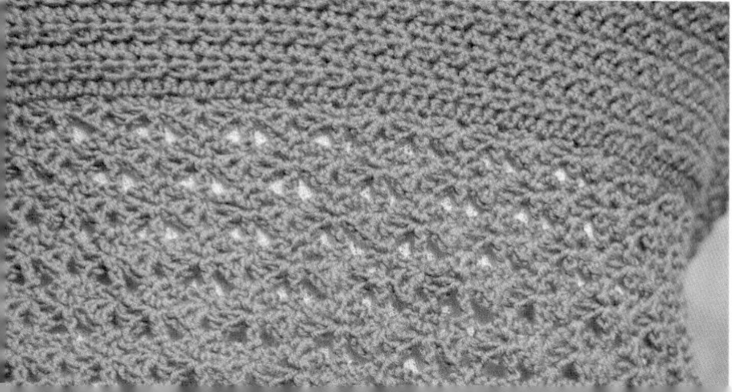

victorian *shrug + wrap*

Robyn Chachula

concentration rating 1 2 3 4

ROBYN'S INSPIRATION

From my insatiable appetite for fashion magazines, I have recently been overcome by all the sexy and confident garments with asymmetrical lines. Yet being a history fan, I always draw inspiration from earlier time periods. For sensual wardrobes, I think back to Victorian times when women wore high necklines and yards of lace. Mixing these two inspirations is how this top was born. A high neckline gives this close-fitting shrug an air of sexy confidence, while an optional addition transforms the shrug into an asymmetrical wrap (see page 29). It's two patterns in one!

FINISHED SIZE

BUST CIRCUMFERENCE: 30 (34, 38, 42)" (76 [87, 97, 107] cm) Sweater is designed to be close-fitting.

YARN

Debbie Bliss Baby Cashmerino (55% merino wool, 33% microfiber, 12% cashmere, 137 yd [125 m]/50 g): color #203. *Shrug:* 6 (7, 8, 9) skeins. *Wrap (page 29):* 11 (12, 14, 15) skeins. Yarn distributed by Knitting Fever.

SUBSTITUTION: About 820 (984, 1,094, 1,312) yd, (750 [900, 1,000, 1,200] m) for the shrug and 1,531 (1,641, 1,914, 2,078) yd, (1,400 [1,500, 1,750, 1,900] m) for the wrap, DK weight (Light #3) cashmere/wool blend yarn.

HOOK

Size G/6 (4.25 mm) hook for body. Size F/5 (3.75 mm) and H/8 (5.0 mm) hook for sleeves. Change hook size if necessary to obtain the correct gauge.

NOTIONS

Yarn needle; two 7/8" (2.2 cm) buttons (one flat and one fancy); sewing needle with matching sewing thread.

GAUGE

22 hdc and 15 rows = 4" (10 cm) in alternating loop stitch pattern (see Special Stitches on page 28) using middle-size hook.

Note: The main body stitch pattern is very elastic. If your gauge is slightly smaller, the garment is still likely to fit, but more snugly.

+ SPECIAL STITCHES +

ALTERNATING LOOP STITCH (ALT LOOP ST PATT): Ch 2 (counts as first hdc), [hdc-flo in each hdc-flo, hdc-blo in each hdc-blo] rep across, hdc in top of tch.

FAN STITCH (FAN ST): (dc, ch 1, dc, ch 3, dc, ch 1, dc) in next st indicated.

LACY STITCH PATTERN

Ch 24, sl st in first ch, turn.

RND 1: Ch 1, sc in first ch, sk 2 ch, fan st in next ch, sk 2 ch, * sc in next ch, sk 2 ch, fan st in next ch, sk 2 ch; rep from * around, sl st in first sc, turn—4 fan sts total.

RND 2: Ch 7 (counts as tr, ch-3 sp), * (sc, ch 3, sc) in ch-3 sp of fan st, ch 3, tr in sc, ch 3; rep from * around, ending (sc, ch3, sc) in ch-3 sp of fan st, ch 3, sl st in 4th ch of beg ch-7, turn.

RND 3: (Ch 4, [counts as dc, ch1], dc, ch 3, dc, ch 1, dc) in same st as join, sk ch-3 sp, sc in next ch-3 sp, * fan st in next tr, sk ch-3 sp, sc in next ch-3 sp; rep from * around, sl st in 3rd ch of beg ch-4, turn.

Rep Rnds 2–3 to desired length.

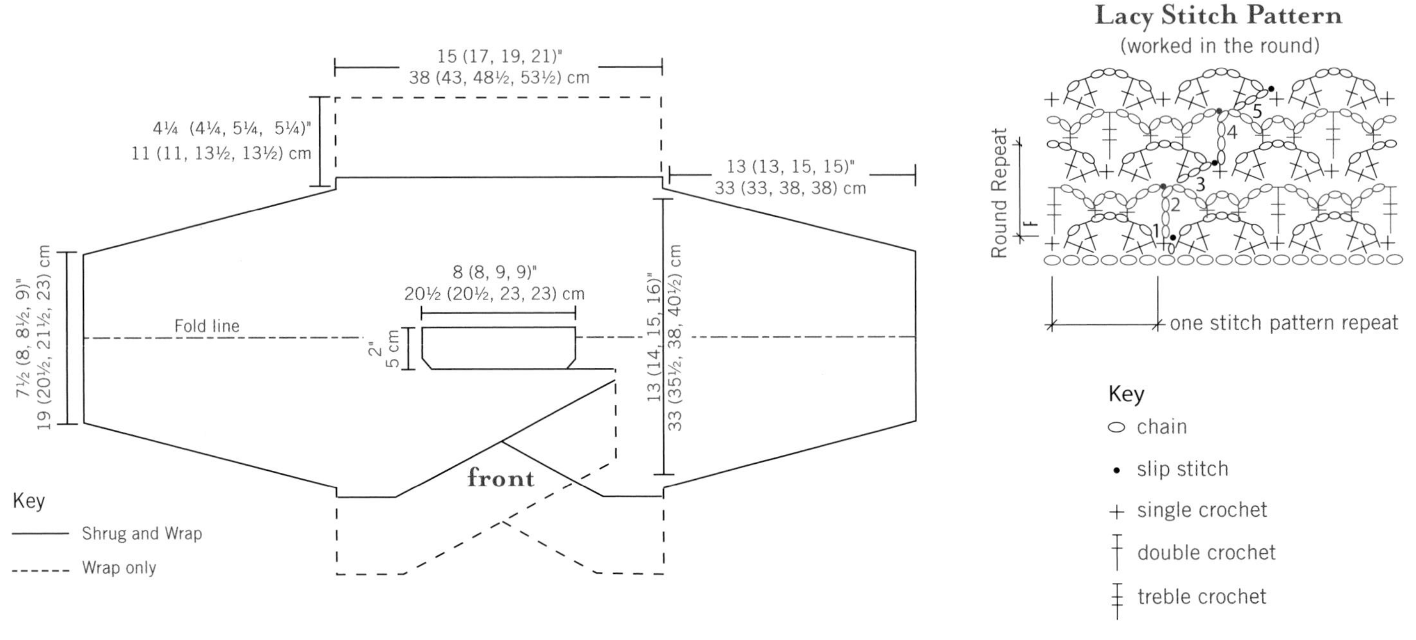

+ PATTERN NOTES +

- The textured stitch made from alternating front loop and back loop half double crochet results in a stretchy fabric.
- The body and sleeves are crocheted in one piece, folded in half, and then lacy cuffs are added.

SHRUG AND WRAP

BACK

With middle-size hook, ch 84 (94, 104, 116).

ROW 1 (RS): Sk first 2 ch (counts as hdc), hdc in each remaining ch, turn—83 (93, 103, 115) hdc total.

ROW 2: Ch 2 (counts as first hdc), [hdc-flo in next st, hdc-blo in next st] rep to last 2 sts, hdc-flo in next st, hdc in top of tch, turn.

FOR SHRUG: Continue to Arm.

FOR WRAP: Work in alt loop st patt (see Special Stitches) until piece measures 4¼ (4¼, 5¼, 5¼)" (11 [11, 13.5, 13.5] cm) from beginning, ending with a WS row.

ARM

ROW 1 (RS): Ch 8 (7, 7, 7), remove hook but do not fasten off, join yarn to opposite end with same hook in top of tch, ch 6 (5, 5, 5). Fasten off. Pick up dropped lp, hdc in 3rd ch from hook (tch counts as hdc), hdc in each ch across, hdc-blo in first hdc of Back, work in alt loop st patt across, hdc in top of tch, hdc in each ch across to last ch, 2 hdc in last ch, turn—97 (105, 115, 127) hdc total.

ROW 2: Rep Row 1—111 (117, 127, 139) hdc total.

ROW 3: Ch 8 (7, 8, 7), remove hook, join yarn to opposite end in top of tch, ch 6 (5, 6, 5). Fasten off. Pick up dropped loop, continue in Row 1 stitch pattern of Arm, turn—125 (129, 141, 151) hdc total.

ROWS 4–6: Rep Row 3—167 (165, 183, 187) hdc total.

ROW 7: Ch 8 (8, 8, 7), remove hook, join yarn to opposite end in top of tch, ch 6 (6, 6, 5). Fasten off. Pick up starting yarn again, continue in Row 1 stitch pattern of Arm—181 (179, 197, 199) hdc total.

ROWS 8–9: Rep Row 7—209 (207, 225, 223) hdc total.

ROW 10: Ch 9 (8, 8, 8), remove hook, join yarn to opposite end in top of tch, ch 7 (6, 6, 6). Fasten off. Pick up starting yarn again, continue in Row 1 stitch pattern of Arm—225 (221, 239, 237) hdc total.

SIZES 34 (38, 42)" (87 [97, 107] CM) ONLY

Rep Row 10 one (two, three) times—235 (267, 279) hdc.

Work even in alt loop st patt for 11 (11, 13, 13) rows.

NECK OPENING

ROW 1 (RS): Ch 2 (counts as first hdc), work in alt loop st patt for 89 (94, 108, 114) hdc, leave remaining hdc unworked, turn—90 (95, 109, 115) hdc total.

ROWS 2–6: Work even in alt loop st patt.

ROW 7: Ch 2 (counts as first hdc), work in alt loop st patt across to last hdc, 2 hdc in top of tch, turn—91 (96, 110, 116) total.

ROW 8: Ch 2, hdc in first hdc (counts as 2 hdc in first st), work in alt loop st patt across, turn—92 (97, 111, 117) hdc total.

ROW 9: Ch 2 (counts as first hdc), remove hook, join yarn to opposite end in top of tch, ch 54 (54, 58, 58). Fasten off. Pick up starting yarn again, work in alt loop st patt across to last hdc, hdc in each ch across, turn—146 (151, 169, 175) hdc total.

RIGHT FRONT PANEL SHAPING

NECK

ROW 1 (WS): Ch 2 (counts as first hdc), work in alt loop st patt for 3 hdc, ch 2 (buttonhole made), sk 2 hdc, work in alt loop st patt across, turn.

SHRUG ONLY

ROW 2: Ch 2 (counts as first hdc), work in alt loop st patt across to buttonhole, 2 hdc in buttonhole, hdc in next hdc, sc in next hdc, sl st in next hdc, leave tch unworked, turn—143 (148, 166, 172) hdc total.

ROW 3: Sk sl st, sl st in sc and each of first 2 hdc, sc in next hdc, work in alt loop st patt across, turn—140 (145, 163, 169) hdc total.

ROW 4: Ch 2 (counts as first hdc), work in alt loop patt st across to last 3 hdc, sc in next hdc, sl st in next hdc, leave tch unworked, turn—137 (142, 160, 166) hdc total.

ROWS 5–9 (9, 11, 11): Rep Rows 3–4 two (two, three, three) times, then rep Row 3 once more—122 (127, 139,145) hdc total.

ARM AND NECK SHAPING

ROW 1: Sl st in each of first 7 (6, 6, 6) hdc, sc in next hdc, work in alt loop st patt across to last 3 hdc, sc in next hdc, sl st in next hdc, leave tch unworked, turn—111 (117, 129, 135) hdc total.

ROW 2: Sl st in sc and first 2 hdc, sc in next hdc, work in alt loop patt st across to last 7 hdc, sc in next hdc, sl st in next hdc, leave remaining hdc unworked, turn—101 (107, 119, 125) hdc total.

ROW 3: Sl st in sc and first 6 hdc, continue as in Row 1 above—91 (97, 109, 115) hdc total.

ROW 4: Rep Row 2—81 (87, 99, 105) hdc total.

ROW 5: Sl st in sc and first 6 (6, 6, 5) hdc, continue as in Row 1 above—71 (77, 89, 97) hdc total.

ROW 6: Rep Row 2 across to last 7 (6, 7, 6) hdc, sc in next hdc, sl st in next hdc, leave remaining hdc unworked, turn—61 (68, 79, 88) hdc total.

ROW 7: Sl st in sc and first 6 (5, 6, 5) hdc,

continue as in Row 1 above—51 (59, 69, 79) hdc total.

ROWS 8–9: Rep Rows 6–7—31 (41, 49, 61) hdc total.

ROW 10: Sl st in sc and first 2 (2, 0, 2) hdc, sc in next hdc, work in alt loop patt st across to last 7 (6, 7, 6) hdc, sc in next hdc, sl st in next hdc, leave remaining hdc unworked, turn—21 (32, 41, 52) hdc total.

SIZE 30" (76 CM) SHRUG ONLY

ROW 11: Ch 1, sc in sc, work in alt loop patt st across to last 3 hdc, sc in next hdc, sl st in next hdc, leave last hdc unworked, turn—18 hdc total.

ROW 12: Sl st in sc and first 2 hdc, sc in next hdc, hdc in each hdc across—15 hdc total. Fasten off.

SIZE 34" (87 CM SHRUG ONLY

ROW 11: Rep Row 7—23 hdc total.

ROW 12: Sl st in sc and first 2 hdc, sc in next hdc, work in alt loop patt st across, turn—20 hdc total.

ROW 13: Ch 2 (counts as first hdc), hdc in each hdc across to last 3 hdc, sc in next hdc, sl st in next hdc, leave last hdc unworked—17 hdc total. Fasten off.

SIZE 38" (97 CM) SHRUG ONLY

ROW 11: Sl st in sc and first 5 hdc, sc in next hdc, work in alt loop patt st across to last hdc, sc in last hdc, turn—34 hdc total.

ROW 12: Sl st in sc, sc in next hdc, work in alt loop patt st across to last 6 hdc, sc in next hdc, sl st in next hdc, leave remaining hdc unworked, turn—27 hdc total.

ROW 13: Ch 1, sc in sc, work in alt loop patt st across to last hdc, sc in last hdc, turn—26 hdc total.

ROW 14: Ch 1, sc in sc, hdc in each hdc across. Fasten off.

SIZE 42" (107 CM) SHRUG ONLY

ROW 11: Rep Row 7—43 hdc total.

ROW 12: Sl st in sc, sc in next hdc, work in alt loop patt st across to last 6 hdc, sc in next hdc, sl st in next hdc, leave remaining hdc unworked, turn—36 hdc total.

ROW 13: Sl st in sc and first 5 hdc, sc in next hdc, work in alt loop patt st across to last hdc, sc in last hdc, turn—29 hdc total.

ROW 14: Sl st in sc, sc in next hdc, work in alt loop patt st across, turn—28 hdc total.

ROW 15: Ch 2 (counts as first hdc), hdc in each hdc across to last hdc, sc in last hdc—27 hdc total. Fasten off.

WRAP ONLY

ROW 2: Ch 2 (counts as first hdc), work in alt loop patt st across to buttonhole, 2 hdc in buttonhole, work in alt loop patt st across, turn—146 (151, 169, 175) hdc total.

ROWS 3–9 (9, 11, 11): Work even in alt loop patt st for 7 (7, 9, 9) rows.

ARM SHAPING

ROW 1: Sl st in first 7 (6, 6, 6) hdc, sc in next hdc, work in alt loop patt st across, turn—138 (144, 162, 168) hdc total.

ROW 2: Ch 2 (counts as first hdc), work in alt loop patt st across to last 7 hdc, sc in next hdc, sl st in next hdc, leave remaining hdc unworked, turn—131 (137, 155, 161) hdc total.

ROW 3: Sl st in first 6 hdc, continue as in Row 1 above, turn—124 (130, 148, 154) hdc total.

ROW 4: Rep Row 2—117 (123, 141, 147) hdc total.

ROW 5: Sl st in first 6 (6, 6, 5) hdc, continue as in Row 1 above—110 (116, 134, 141) hdc total.

ROW 6: Follow Row 2 until last 7 (6, 7, 6) hdc, sc in next hdc, sl st in next hdc, leave remaining hdc unworked, turn—103 (110, 127, 135) hdc total.

SIZES 38 (42)" (97 [107] CM) WRAP ONLY

Rep Rows 5–6 once—113 (123) hdc total.

NECK SHAPING

ROW 1: Sl st in first 6 (5, 6, 5) hdc, sc in next hdc, work in alt loop patt st across to last 3 hdc, sc in next hdc, sl st in next hdc, leave last hdc unworked, turn—93 (101, 103, 114) hdc total.

ROW 2: Sl st in sc and first 2 hdc, sc in next hdc, work in alt loop patt st across to last 7 (6, 7, 6) hdc, sc in next hdc, sl st in next hdc, leave remaining hdc unworked, turn—83 (92, 93, 105) hdc total.

ROW 3: Sl st in first 6 (5, 5, 5) hdc, continue with Row 1—73 (83, 84, 96) hdc total.

ROW 4: Rep Row 2 across to last 7 (6, 6, 6) hdc, sc in next hdc, sl st in next hdc, leave remaining hdc unworked, turn—63 (74, 75, 87) hdc total.

SIZES 30 (38)" (76 [97] CM) WRAP ONLY

ROW 5: Ch 1, sc in sc, work in alt loop patt st across to last 3 hdc, sc in next hdc, sl st in next hdc, leave last hdc unworked, turn—60 (72) hdc total.

SIZES 34 (42)" (87 [107] CM WRAP ONLY

ROW 5: Sl st in first 5 (5) hdc, continue as in Row 1, turn—65 (78) hdc total.

ALL SIZES

ROW 6: Sl st in sc and first 2 hdc, sc in next hdc, work in alt loop patt st across, turn—57 (62, 69, 75) hdc total.

ROW 7: Ch 2 (counts as first hdc), work in alt loop patt st across to last 3 hdc, sc in next hdc, sl st in next hdc, leave last hdc unworked, turn—54 (59, 66, 72) hdc total.

ROWS 8–19 (19, 19, 21): Rep Rows 6–7 6 (6, 6, 7) times—18 (23, 30, 30) hdc total.

SIZE 30" (76 CM) WRAP ONLY

ROW 20: Sl st in sc and first 2 hdc, sc in next hdc, hdc in each hdc across—15 hdc total. Fasten off.

SIZE 34" (87 CM) WRAP ONLY

ROW 20: Rep Row 6—20 hdc total.

ROW 21: Ch 2 (counts as first hdc), hdc in each hdc across to last 3 hdc, sc in next hdc, sl st in next hdc, leave last hdc unworked—17 hdc total. Fasten off.

SIZES 38 (42)" (97 [107] CM) WRAP ONLY

ROW 20 (22): Sl st in sc, sc in next hdc, work in alt loop patt st across, turn—29 hdc total.

ROW 21 (23): Ch 2 (counts as first hdc), work in alt loop patt st across to last hdc, sc in last hdc, turn—28 hdc total.

ROW 22 (24): Rep Rows 20–21—26 hdc total.

SIZE 38" (97 CM) WRAP ONLY

ROW 23: Rep Row 21—25 hdc total.

ROW 24: Ch 1, sc in sc, hdc in each hdc across. Fasten off.

SIZE 42" (107 CM) WRAP ONLY

ROW 25: Ch 2 (counts as hdc), hdc in each hdc across to last hdc, sc in last hdc. Fasten off.

LEFT FRONT PANEL

Join yarn with middle-size hook 45 (45, 49, 49) hdc from last hdc in Row 1 of neck opening.

Ch 2. Follow neck and panel directions above, reversing all shaping. Fasten off.

FINISHING

Weave in yarn ends. Fold shrug in half with right sides together. With yarn needle and matching yarn, whipstitch arm and side seams. Turn right sides out, line up front panels. Sew buttons to top shoulder with small needle and matching thread on each side, see picture for assistance.

BOTTOM EDGING

SHRUG ONLY: Using middle-size hook and with right side facing, join yarn to bottom of front panel, ch 1, sc evenly around front panel and neck opening. Fasten off. Weave in ends.

WRAP ONLY: With RS facing and middle-size hook, join yarn to bottom of front panel, ch 2, hdc 64 (69, 67, 73) times evenly along diagonal edge, sc evenly along vertical edge and neck opening, hdc 64 (69, 67, 73) times evenly along diagonal edge. Fasten off. Weave in ends.

CUFFS

With RS facing and smallest hook, join yarn to cuff at arm seam.

Ch 2 (counts as hdc), hdc 47 (53, 59, 65) times evenly around cuff, sl st in tch, turn.

RND 1: Ch 1, [sc in hdc, sk 2 hdc, fan st in next hdc, sk 2 hdc] rep around, sl st in first sc, turn—8 (9, 10, 11) fan sts total.

Work Rnds 2 and 3 of lacy st patt (see Special Stitches) for 8 rounds, switching to middle-size hook on 2nd round, then switch to largest hook on 6th round. Rep Rnd 2 once.

Fasten off. Weave in ends.

LACY TOP EDGING, WRAP ONLY

With RS facing and smallest hook, join yarn to front panel at diagonal edge.

ROW 1: Ch 1, sc in first hdc, sk next 2 hdc, fan st (see Special Stitches) in next hdc, * sc in next hdc, sk next 2 hdc, fan st in next hdc, sk next 2 hdc; sk next 2 hdc, rep from * around front panel diagonal edges and back, end with sc, turn—20 (22, 24, 26) fan sts total.

ROW 2: Ch 7 (counts as tr, ch-3 sp), * (sc, ch 3, sc) in ch-3 sp of fan st, ch 3, tr in sc, ch 3; rep from * across, end with tr in last sc, turn.

ROW 3: Switch to middle-size hook, (ch 4, dc, ch 1, dc) in first tr (half fan st made), sk ch-3 sp, sc in next ch-3 sp, * fan st in next tr, sk, ch-3 sp, sc in next ch-3 sp; rep from * across to last tr, (dc, ch 1, dc, ch1, dc) in last tr, turn.

ROW 4: Ch 1, sc in dc, sc in ch-1 sp, ch 3, tr in sc, ch 3, * (sc, ch 3, sc) in ch-3 sp, ch 3, tr in sc, ch 3; rep from * across to half fan st, sk ch-1 sp, sc in 4th ch of tch, turn.

ROW 5: Ch 1, sc in sc, * fan st in next tr, sk ch-3 sp, sc in next ch-3 sp; rep from * across to last tr, sc in last sc, turn.

Rep Rows 2–5—3 (4, 5, 5) times or to desired length.

Rep Row 2 once. Fasten off. Weave in ends.

technically speaking: READING STITCH DIAGRAMS

Now, dear readers, take a deep breath and mentally embrace the crochet symbol. The symbol is a thing of elegance. In one line drawing you get all the information contained in a paragraph of frighteningly complex abbreviations and punctuation. As an added bonus, the diagram even closely resembles the fabric you'll create.

As with color charts, you begin following the symbols in the lower right. Each row is marked with a number. Odd-numbered rows are read from right to left, even-numbered rows from left to right. Symbols depicting crochet in the round are followed from the center out and are read in a counterclockwise direction. Every time a symbol diagram is used, a key accompanies it to show you what each symbol stands for. For example, the diagram below from the Comfy Cardi on page 90 gives you all the information you need to crochet a lacy stitch pattern.

It's possible, even likely, that you've never followed a symbol diagram before. If you hate following a text pattern, symbols will be your salvation. And you'll be seeing symbol diagrams more and more in crochet publications and text less and less. So get used to it. Also, get used to the world growing ever smaller as your newfound symbol skills allow you to follow crochet patterns from foreign publications in French, Dutch, or Japanese or some other unfamiliar language. The beauty of crochet symbols is they are universal.

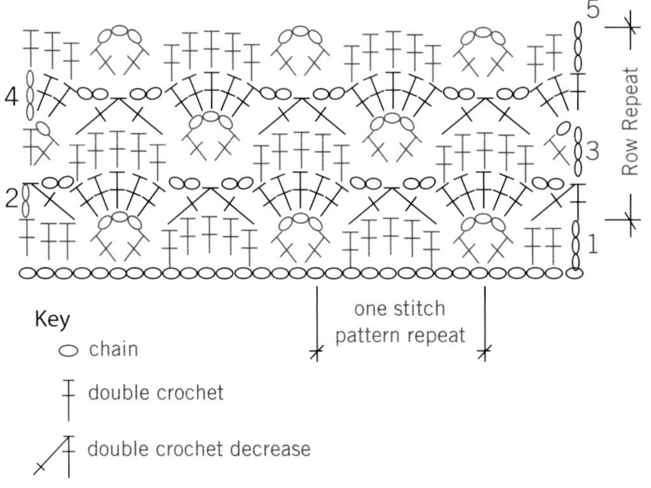

PHOTO BY MARK CHACHULA.

designer in profile

robyn chachula

Robyn has a huge German Shepherd named Faye. Robyn designs under the label *Crochet by Faye*. Clearly, it's Robyn doing the crocheting and not Faye. Other than this—trying to pass off her dog as a crocheter, (silly Robyn)—her approach to crochet is so sensible and so strong that it's something I simply love to watch.

Not surprisingly, Robyn's first published crochet pattern was a simple leash and poop bag (take a guess at her inspiration) in the Summer 2005 issue of CrochetMe.com. After that it was like watching a switch flip: Suddenly Robyn was designing gorgeous garments and her work started appearing in publications industry-wide. A structural engineer by day, she has a talent for crochet garment construction.

Despite her penchant for hanging off the sides of buildings as part of her day job, Robyn's a scaredy-cat when it comes to movies, preferring indie rom-coms to horror flicks. She has a collection of messy crafty clothes at home to safeguard against the messes she creates when she does stuff like paint walls, make furniture, or quilt. But her exceptional crafting skills are tested with knitting. Robyn's such a slow knitter it's painful to watch. Or so she says; I've never watched her knit.

In her own words, here's what Robyn has to say about the renaissance of crafts among the career-oriented in our generation: "I think the resurgence in the last few years does fit into larger social issues. I think there are a lot of folks my age who are heavily career-oriented and do not feel like they really were groomed in any home skills, such as cooking, sewing, cleaning, or crafting. And one day, it just made me sad to think that my family's history and possibly craft itself may be lost, because I and a lot of other young people were not promoting and continuing it. So I got off my butt (as did a ton of others), and we (in my mind at least) are making history. Saying that yes, you can be a professional whatever by day and a cooking/sewing/crafting fool by night."

HANG OUT WITH ROBYN AT CROCHETBYFAYE.COM.

mini *wrap skirt*

Amy O'Neill Houck

concentration rating 1 2 3 4

AMY'S INSPIRATION

When creating this skirt, I was inspired by Mia, my son's hip, vegan, bike-commuting babysitter. She wears little miniskirts over her (often striped) leggings, which lets her look cool while riding her bike and playing with kids. I wanted something with the same sort of edginess, so I chose black and claret. I wanted durability and Red Heart yarn makes this a skirt that can stand up to any activity. This project is great for scarf makers who want to branch out—it's fun and fast to make and requires no special shaping techniques. It's just a rectangle!

FINISHED SIZE

32 (34, 38, 44)" (81.5 [86.5, 96.5, 112] cm) at high hip bone. *Note:* This is your circumference right at the hip bone, and it's where the skirt is designed to sit. If you want your skirt to sit higher on your waist, measure there. *Waistband:* 44 (46, 50, 56)" (112 [117, 127, 142] cm). *Wrap skirt circumference:* 54 (56, 58, 64)" (137 [142, 147.5, 162.5] cm). *Length (excluding edging):* 13 (14, 15, 17)" (33 [35.5, 38, 43] cm).

YARN

Red Heart Super Saver (100% acrylic, 364 yd [333 m]/198 g), # 378 black (MC), 2 skeins, and #312 Claret (CC), 1 skein. Yarn distributed by Coats and Clark.

SUBSTITUTION: About 550 (550, 600, 650) yd (503 [503, 549, 594] m) worsted-weight (Medium #4) yarn.

HOOK

Size H/8 (5mm) for waistband and size J/10 (6.0 mm) for skirt. Change hook size if necessary to obtain the correct gauge.

NOTIONS

Yarn needle, 2 buttons sized to fit through the holes of your waistband fabric and 2 buttons sized to fit through the holes of your skirt fabric.

GAUGE

Waistband: 18 sc-blo and 11 rows = 4" (10 cm) with smaller hook. *Skirt:* 10.5 hdc and 8.5 rows = 4" (10 cm) with larger hook.

+ SPECIAL STITCHES +

CROSSED TREBLE STITCH (CROSSED TR ST): *Sk next 2 sts, tr in next st, crossing over the front of the tr just worked: tr into 2nd skipped st, ch 1; rep from * across.

SC-BLO: Sc through back loop only.

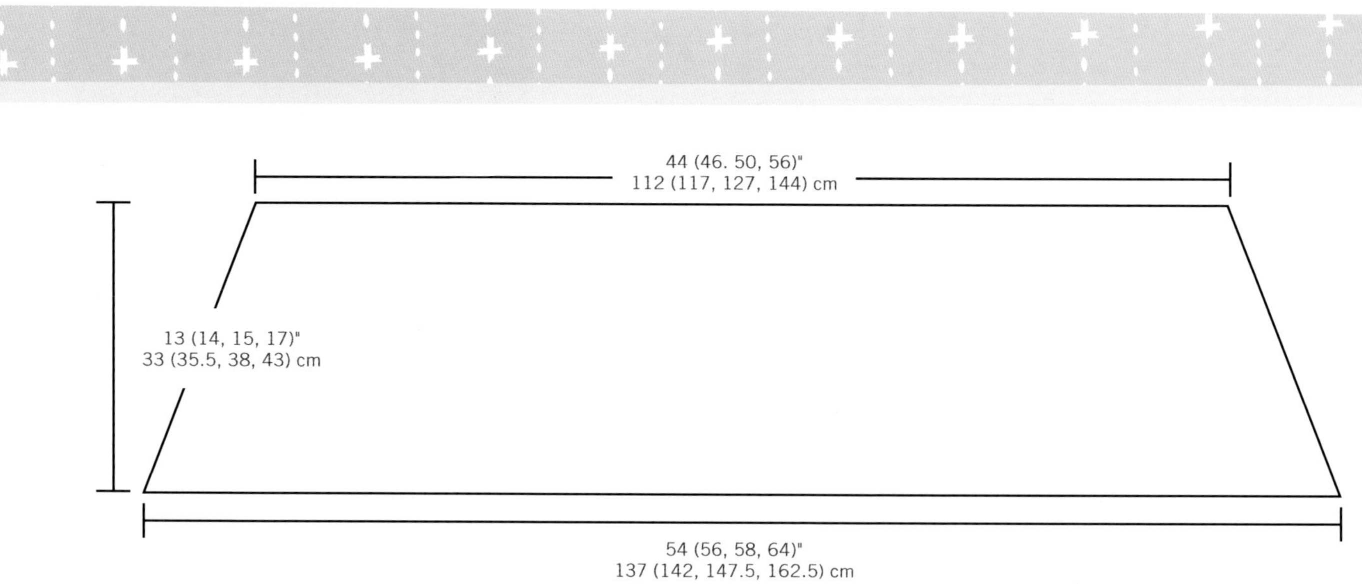

WAISTBAND

The waistband is worked from side to side. If you want a thicker band, adjust as necessary by adding or subtracting foundation chains.

Using CC and smaller hook, ch 11.

ROW 1: Sc in 2nd ch and in each ch across, turn—10 sc.

ROW 2: Ch 1, sc-blo (see Special Stitches) in each st across, turn.

Rep Row 2 for 44 (46, 50, 56)" (112 [117, 127, 142] cm).

Fasten off.

SKIRT

FOUNDATION ROW: With MC and smaller hook, and working into the end of each row along the waistband, join yarn in first row, ch 1, sc into the end of each row, turn.

ROW 1: Switch to larger hook, ch 1, sc in each st across, turn.

ROW 2: Ch 2 (does not count as st), hdc in each st across, do not hdc in turning ch, turn.

Repeat Row 2 until skirt is 13 (14, 15, 17)" (33 [35.5, 38, 43] cm) from beginning or is desired length.

Note: When trying on the skirt, pay attention to the length in back since it's likely to sit a bit higher than in front.

Fasten off.

EDGING

Join CC at beg of next row, ch 4 (counts as tr), work in crossed tr st patt (see Special Stitches) until there are 3 sts left, sk 2 sts, tr in last st.

Fasten off.

FINISHING

Weave in yarn ends. Avoiding the waistband, lightly steam-block the skirt. Hold the steamer or steam iron 8–10" (20.5–25.5 cm) from the fabric, taking care not to overdo it because acrylic yarn doesn't take heat very well. Lightly steaming the skirt will work wonders for its texture and drape. (See Block It sidebar on page 66.)

BUTTONS

Sew two buttons, one above the other, ½" (1.3 cm) from edge of waistband on one short side. These will be the inside buttons. Try the skirt on overlapping the front and sew two more buttons onto waistband just under second flap edge (about 12" [30.5 cm] in from the first set). You can button the skirt with all four buttons buttoned into the stitches of the waist-band or with the two edge buttons buttoned into the skirt fabric for an asymmetrical look.

ESSAY: a different kind of post

I'm often asked why crochet in particular, and needle arts in general, are currently so popular. Sometimes the question is posed specifically about people in my generation (I usually interpret that to mean members of Gen X, who are for the most part older than I am, and Gen Y, who are younger). There are several accepted theories that come to mind.

I mention the theory that in our post-9/11 world, people have come back to valuing home and family more than they have in decades, and so the "home arts" are resurging in popularity. And I particularly like the theory that in a material world consisting overwhelmingly of mass-produced items manufactured under mysterious if not downright shady circumstances, we're coming back to valuing artisanship and a DIY approach. I'll admit this reason informs much of my own fascination with making things and my preference for buying handmade goods.

My pet theory, though, is one that hits home only slightly more than the mass-production theory. It's the post-feminist theory. Not "post-feminist" in the sense that I think feminism is dead (au contraire). Just "post-feminist" in the post-second-wave feminism sense. In my mind, the post-feminist theory of our lovely crafty revolution is that fiber arts are popular these days because we're reclaiming the "women's work" from which our mothers fought so hard to break free.

I grew up eyeing my mom's copy of *Ms.* magazine on the coffee table. My mom was a union activist practically from the day she started teaching in Crown Heights at barely twenty-one to the day she retired a couple of years ago. I grew up talking politics at the dinner table, encouraged to question everything and to challenge when it was appropriate.

My mom didn't teach me to crochet, knit, or sew. I figured out how to sew on a button out of necessity when I was in college. When I was growing up, my mom worked from early in the morning until after my brother and I got home from school, then she made dinner and graded papers until she fell asleep at night. She taught me about power relations, racism, sexism, ethnocentrism, and activism.

I very much appreciate that I was handed every opportunity to pursue whatever dream I had at the moment. When my teenage aspirations of changing the world through medicine, law, or government morphed silently into my early adult confusion and meandering, my parents always supported my decisions, even the bad ones.

Oh,the delight my mom took when I signed my first book contract! The hilarity that I, the child of a braless second-wave feminist, finally had a career and that the career was crochet was lost on no one.

At no point has the following been lost on me: I broke rules, tried a multitude of jobs, and started something new (CrochetMe.com) because my parents taught me how to be an activist and to value creation, ingenuity, the opinions of others, and myself.

I like to crochet and knit because I find it personally satisfying. But it also ties me to all the generations of women who came before me. I have absolutely no knowledge of my family before my great-grandparents. I can only imagine that the way my hands move fiber today is the same way my nameless, faceless ancestors' hands moved fiber. I don't crochet and knit because I have to. I do it because I want to. And that, quite simply, is a very post-feminist thing to say.

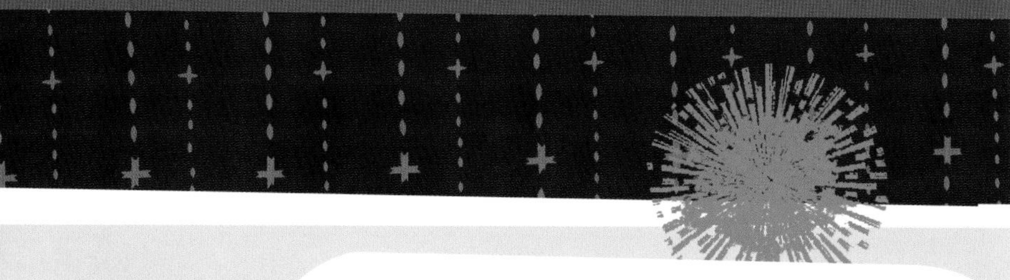

messenger *bag*

Julie Armstrong Holetz

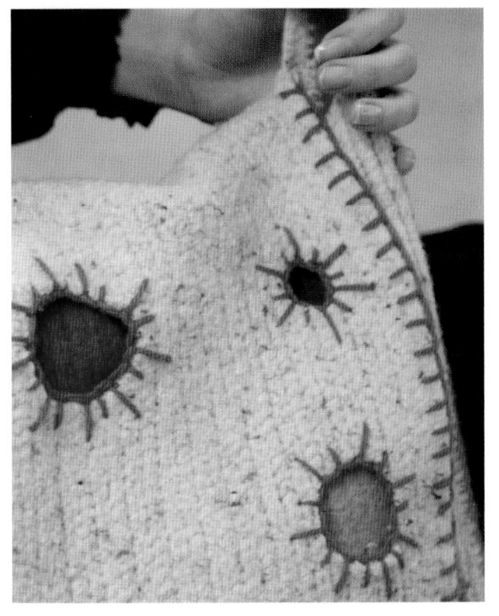

concentration rating 1 **2** 3 4

JULIE'S INSPIRATION

I wanted to create a design that could be adapted easily to make something unique. The construction of the bag is very simple; it's what you do with it that makes it special. By making changes to the cut-out design or embroidered edging or by changing colors, you can give this bag a whole new personality. If you don't want to do the color blocks but like the idea of a contrast color showing through the holes, simply make the bag in one color, cut out the holes, and line the flap in a contrasting color.

FINISHED SIZE

BEFORE FELTING:
20" (51 cm) wide, 19¼" (49 cm) high, 4¾" (12 cm) deep.

AFTER FELTING:
15" (38 cm) wide, 12" (30.5 cm) high, 3" (7.5 cm) deep.

YARN

Cascade 220 Tweed (90% wool, 10% Donegal; 220 yd [201 m]/100 g): #615 ck white, 5 skeins (MC); #9465B dark orange, 2 skeins (CC1); #9430 dark green, 1 skein (CC2); #2413 red, 1 skein (CC3); #7825 light orange, 1 skein (CC4).

SUBSTITUTION: About 1,350 yd (1,234 m) worsted-weight (Medium #4) 100% wool. Do not use superwash wool.

HOOK

Size I/9 (5.5 mm) and J/10 (6 mm). Change hook size if necessary to obtain the correct gauge.

NOTIONS

Straight pins; large yarn needle; stitch markers (optional); 20 yd (18 m) scrap cotton yarn, worsted weight or lighter; pillowcase for felting (use either a zippered pillowcase or a regular case with a thick rubber band to close); baking soda; sharp scissors.

GAUGE

12 hdc and 10 rows = 4" (10 cm) with smaller hook before felting.

+ PATTERN NOTES +

- The body of the bag is worked in one piece, making up the front, bottom, back, and flap. The sides and strap are worked separately as one piece, then stitched to the bag before felting.
- Using a larger hook for the foundation chain will keep the foundation edge from becoming narrower than the rest of the panel after felting.

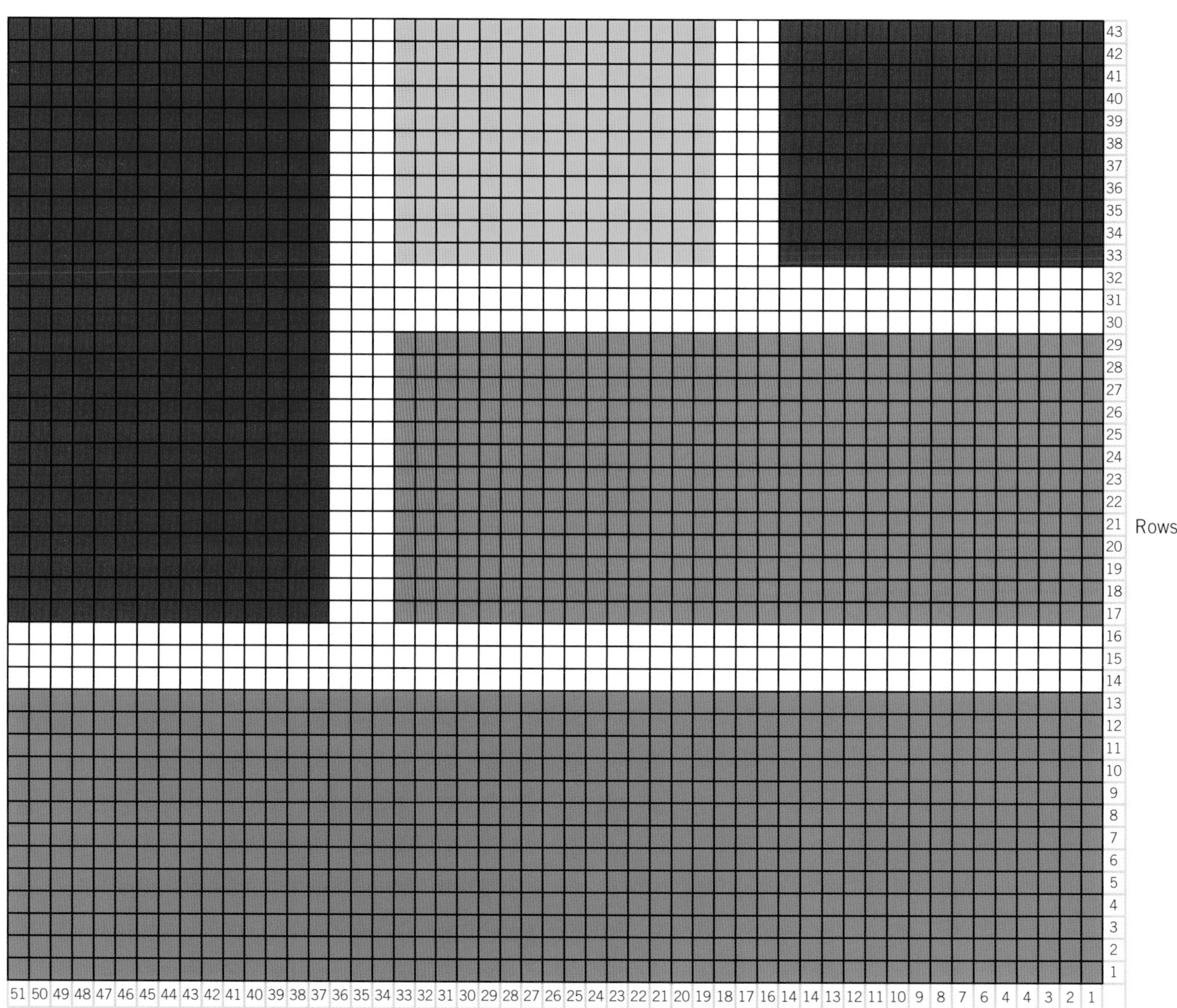

- The color block chart is worked over the first 57 sts of the row when the RS is facing and over the last 57 sts when the WS is facing. Work the remainder of the row in MC only.
- The turning chain does not count as a stitch throughout pattern.
- Don't worry about weaving in the loose ends too perfectly. Any tail ends can be snipped off after everything is felted and dry.
- Any unsecured edges of the bag will stretch during the felting process causing the edges to be uneven with the seamed edges. Stretching will also occur with pieces of crocheted fabric that are considerably longer in one direction versus another, such as the strap. One way to make edges felt more evenly is to loosely baste the edges and openings with a cotton thread or yarn. You will remove the basting thread after washing, and any visible holes can be quickly "erased" by hand felting with hot water. (See Finishing section for more information.)

BAG

BODY

Follow chart for color changes.

With larger hook and MC, ch 195.

ROW 1 (RS): Switch to smaller hook and begin chart, hdc in 2nd ch from hook, hdc in each ch across, turn—194 hdc.

ROW 2: Ch 1, hdc in first st, hdc in each st across, turn.

ROWS 3–51: Rep Row 2 until piece measures 20" (51 cm) while following color chart. Fasten off.

STRAP

With larger hook and MC, ch 291.

ROW 1: Switch to smaller hook, hdc in 2nd ch from hook, hdc in each ch across, turn—290 hdc.

ROW 2: Ch 1, hdc in first st, hdc in each st across, turn.

ROWS 3–13: Rep Row 2, working 3 rows in MC, 6 rows in CC1, then 2 rows in MC.

ROW 14: Ch 1, sc in each st across.

Fasten off.

FINISHING

Weave in yarn ends.

ASSEMBLY

Using straight pins as markers, start at the color block edges, placing markers on both edges at 19¼" (49 cm) and 24" (61 cm) to mark the front and back edge of the bottom panel. Place markers on both edges at 19¼" (49 cm) from each short end of the Strap. With WS held together, center the ends of the Strap between the markers on each side of the Body and pin into place. Using Strap markers to mark the beginning and end of the seam and leaving 19¼" (49 cm) of the Body unattached for the flap, pin Straps to Body. With MC and smaller hook, sc sides of Strap to the Body. Fasten off and weave in ends. Remove pins.

BASTING

With a yarn needle threaded with cotton yarn, loosely baste the opening of the bag closed. Fold the flap over the front panel. With each side flush to the edges of the bag, baste all three edges of the flap to the bag. Fold the strap of the bag in half, then fold in half again and baste through all layers.

FELTING

Place the bag into the pillowcase and zip or secure with a thick rubber band to avoid clumps of wool fuzzies from clogging up your machine. Set the washing machine for a small load with hot water. Toss the pillowcase in with ¼ c (2 oz) of baking soda or mild detergent and a pair of jeans (for agitation) and wash. Stop the washer periodically to check the progress of the felting. With each cycle the bag will shrink more and more. Without letting the washer go to the spin cycle, repeat wash cycles until the bag has felted to measurements. If you don't see a significant change after the first three cycles, you can make the water hotter by adding a pot of boiling water, increase agitation by throwing in a tennis ball, or allow it to go to a cold rinse cycle (but don't let it go to spin!). When the bag has reached the desired size, lay it out flat on a towel and roll the towel to remove as much water as possible. The bag may appear out of shape in some areas. Snip and remove the basting yarn. Pull and stretch the bag to the desired shape, making sure the flap is even with the width of the bag. Insert a plastic form (I use phone books covered in plastic grocery bags) to help the bag keep its shape while drying. Pin the flap to the edge of the front panel. Allow the bag to completely air-dry, possibly overnight or longer.

CUTOUTS AND EMBROIDERY

The flap may have stretched during the wash. Using sharp scissors, trim the flap so the bottom edge is even with the front panel of the bag. Using blanket stitch (see below) and CC1, stitch around the three open sides of the flap. Carefully cut 1–2" (2–2.5 cm) holes over various color blocks as pictured and blanket-stitch around the holes. Weave in ends.

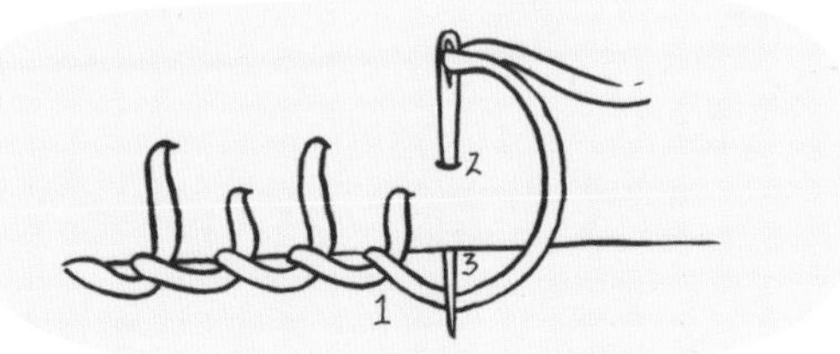

LONG AND SHORT BLANKET STITCH

Working from left to right, bring the needle up at 1 and insert at 2. Bring back up at 3 and over the working thread. Repeat by making the next stitch about twice as long as the stitch that runs from 1 to 2. Note: Regular blanket stitch is achieved by keeping the distance between 2 and 3 consistent.

PHOTO BY STEVEN HOLETZ

designer in profile

julie armstrong holetz

Since I started CrochetMe.com, I've received a surprising amount of e-mail. You'd be amazed by the things people dream up to write to a perfect stranger, and occasionally a message rubs me the wrong way. But not the e-mail I got one day from Julie. It was long. It was funny. It was well-written. She volunteered to help with the site. I was so intrigued that I let the e-mail sit in my Inbox for a couple of months while I tried to figure out how to take her up on her offer. Turns out all I had to do was write her back (this was an important and obvious lesson for me). My eventual reply just might have been the snowflake that got the avalanche of CrochetMe.com underway. Julie's entree into CrochetMe-land had several major ramifications. Most significant was that I no longer ran the site from the solitude of my own head. I'm an ideas person; I thrive on brainstorming and critiquing, poking holes and poking fun. Now I had someone who wasn't my husband to talk to about things. Also, Julie tech-edited the patterns, which saved me a huge amount of time.

Furthermore, Julie's a fabulous designer. "Once I published my first pattern," she said, "I figured it was safe to call myself a designer, but I really consider myself more of a pattern writer. I think it takes finesse to be able to communicate exactly how a project should be worked in order for it to become the photo sample." She's so right.

Julie grew up a L.A. roller-skating diva (she mentions *Xanadu*), and she now makes her home in suburban Washington State. She loves movies of all sorts, and I hear her home could pass for a bookstore. It could also pass for a kiddy-craft heaven, where she makes all sorts of fun stuff with her two kids. Glitter, glue, sequins, and foamies are never far from underfoot. Although she's not a big fan of ribbon yarns, Julie will crochet with pretty much anything else: cotton, rayon, wool, raffia, leather, and string licorice.

In addition to writing a book to teach kids how to crochet (*Crochet Away!*), Julie teaches real live kids how to crochet. "It's never too late to learn to crochet and it's almost never too early," she says. "Kids can be exposed to fiber arts as young as ages four to six. Starting them off early with finger crochet is ideal because it gets them working with the yarn right away and helps promote dexterity. Then, when they reach ages six to eight, children are able to begin working with a crochet hook and it becomes a fun way to learn math, design, and yarn stashing. Oh, and don't forget about the boys! In my experience, boys love to learn crochet as much as girls."

KEEP TABS ON JULIE AT SKAMAMA.COM.

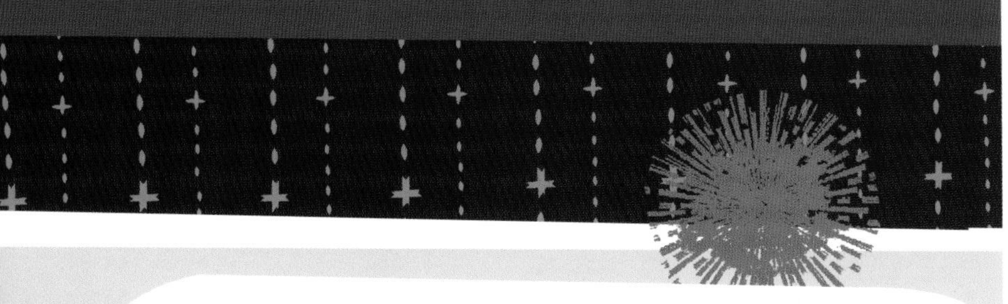

i'm a convert *sweater*

Missa Hills

concentration rating 1 **2** 3 4

MISSA'S INSPIRATION

I wanted a sweater I could wear in almost any season. As I was drawing up the shape for this pullover, I realized I could get a design that was modular: Take the sleeves off, rip off the neck piece, and you have a spring T-shirt! The yarn itself helped with the shaping of the top to create a tight, stretchy fit in single crochet worked in the front loop only. Not only is the sweater modular, it has an open-work stitch designed to be worn over a shirt, camisole, or alone for a cool breeze!

FINISHED SIZE

BUST CIRCUMFERENCE: 30–32 (34–36, 38–40, 40–42)" (76–81.5 [86.5–91.5, 96.5–101.5, 101.5–106.5] cm). This pullover is very stretchy. The actual finished size will measure smaller when lying flat.

YARN

Rowan RY Cashsoft DK (50% extra-fine merino, 40% acrylic microfiber, 10% cashmere, 146 yd [130 m]/ 50 g): #523 lichen (MC), 8 (9, 10, 11) skeins and # 513 poison (CC) 1 (1, 2, 2) skein(s). Yarn distributed by Westminster Fibers.

SUBSTITUTION: About 1,040 (1,160, 1,260, 1,400) yd (951 [1,061, 1,152, 1,280] m) DK weight (Light #3) stretchy yarn.

HOOK

Size H/8 (5.0 mm). Change hook size if necessary to obtain the correct gauge.

NOTIONS

Yarn needle.

GAUGE

22 sts and 12 rows = 4" (10 cm) in (ch 1, sk 1, 1 sc-flo) pattern.

Note: Because you are working into the front loop of the stitches, your rows will be taller than usual and very stretchy. When measuring gauge, stretch the fabric out a bit first before measuring.

+ SPECIAL STITCHES +

PATTERN STITCH (PATT ST)

ROW 1: Sc in 2nd ch from hook (skipped ch counts as tch), [ch 1, sk 1 ch, sc in next ch] across, turn.

ROW 2: Ch 1 (counts as a tch), working in the flo here and throughout, sc in next st, [ch 1, sk 1 st, sc-flo in next st], ending with sc-flo in tch, turn.

Rep Row 2 for pattern.

SC-FLO: Work sc in front lp only.

HDC-FLO: Work hdc in front lp only.

DC-FLO: Work dc in front lp only.

SINGLE CROCHET FRONT LOOP ONLY CLUSTER (SC-FLO CL): Insert hook in front lp of next st, yo, draw up lp, sk next st, insert hook in front lp of next ch, yo, draw up lp, yo, draw through all 3 lps on hook.

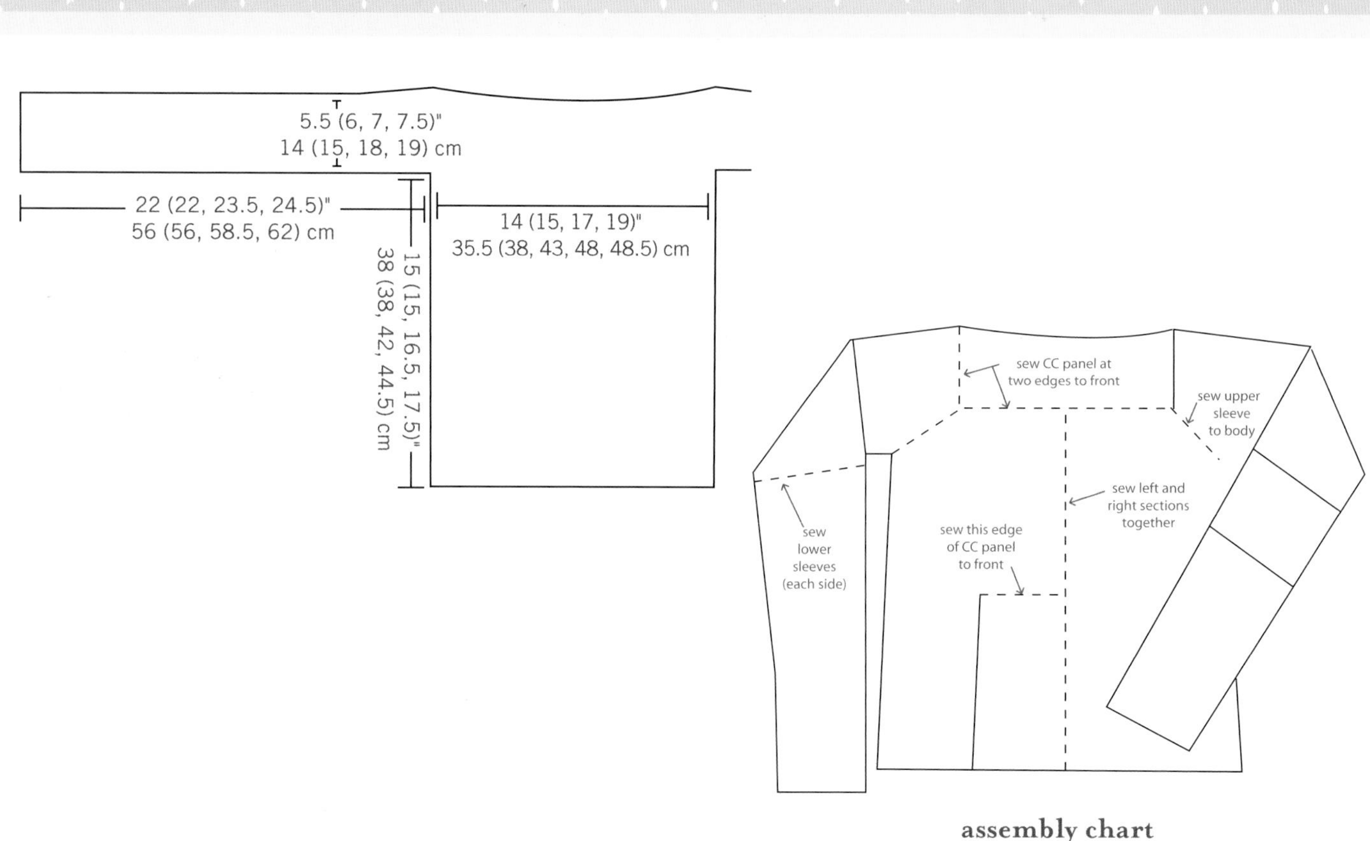

assembly chart

+ PATTERN NOTES +

- All stitches are worked through the *front loop* of the stitch in the previous row. Count the single crochets and the turning chains as stitches.
- The sweater is worked side to side for the front and back; each is made of two pieces sewn together. This gives the width of the sweater a lot of stretch.
- You can place a half double crochet row anywhere within the pattern to make the style your own. You can use up to 2 hdc rows in each half section and still keep the pattern true to size.
- Ch-1 at beginning of rows counts as a stitch. The last stitch worked in each row will be worked into the turning chain of previous row.

SWEATER

FRONT LEFT

Beginning at side, with MC, ch 74 (74, 78, 82).

ROW 1: Sk first ch from hook (counts as tch here and throughout), sc in next ch, *ch 1, sk 1 ch, sc in next ch; rep from * across, turn—74 (74, 78, 82) sts, incl tch.

ROW 2: Ch 1, sc-flo (see Special Stitches) in next ch, * ch 1, sk 1 st, sc-flo in next ch; rep from * ending with sc-flo in tch, turn.

ROW 3 (INCREASE ROW): Ch 5, sk first ch from hook (counts as tch), sc in next ch, ch 1, sk 1 ch, sc in next ch, ch 1, skip next ch and sc, sc-flo in next ch, * ch 1, sk 1 st, sc-flo in next ch; repeat from * ending with sc-flo in tch, turn—78 (78, 82, 86) sts, incl tch.

ROW 4: Ch 1, sc-flo in next ch, * ch 1, sk 1 st, sc-flo in next ch; rep from * ending with sc-flo in tch, turn.

ROW 5 (INCREASE ROW): Ch 3, sk first ch from hook, sc in next ch, ch 1, sk next ch and sc, sc-flo in next ch, * ch 1, sk 1 st, sc-flo in next ch; repeat from * ending with sc-flo in tch, turn—80 (80, 84, 88) sts, incl tch.

ROWS 6–9 (9, 13, 13): Rep Rows 4 and 5 two (two, four, four) times—84 (84, 92, 96) sts, incl tch.

Work even in patt st (see Special Stitches) for three rows.

NEXT ROW: Ch 2 (counts as tch), hdc-flo (see Special Stitches) in next ch, * ch 1, sk 1 st, hdc-flo in next ch; rep from * ending with hdc-flo in tch, turn. Work even in patt st for 9 (11, 11, 13) rows or until piece measures 7 (8, 9, 9½)" (18 [20.5, 23, 24] cm) from beginning.

Fasten off.

FRONT RIGHT

Work as for Front Left through Row 12 (12, 16, 16).

ROW 1: Ch 1, sc-flo in next ch, * ch 1, sk 1 st, sc-flo in next ch; rep from * 21 times, turn—44 (44, 44, 44) sts, incl tch.

Work even in patt st for 4 rows.

NEXT ROW: Ch 2, hdc-flo in next ch, * ch 1, sk 1 st, hdc-flo in next ch; rep from * ending with hdc-flo in tch, turn. Work even in patt st until piece measures 7 (8, 9, 9½)" (18 [20.5, 23, 24] cm) from beginning of panel or measures even with Front Left.

Fasten off MC. With WS facing, join CC with a sl st to inside corner stitch of Row 12 (12, 16, 16) (where you turned to create a short row); you will be working along MC row from the center towards the bottom edge.

ROW 1: Ch 1, sc-flo in next ch, * ch 1, sk 1 st, sc-flo in next ch; rep from * ending with sc-flo in tch, turn.

ROW 2: Ch 3, dc-flo (see Special Stitches) in next ch, * ch 1, sk 1 st, dc-flo in next ch; rep from * ending with dc-flo in tch, turn.

Continue in patt st, working 1 row of dc-flo, 1 row of sc-flo, 3 (4, 5, 6) rows of dc-flo, and 1 row of sc-flo.

Fasten off.

BACK HALF

(Make 2)

Work as for Front Left.

SLEEVES

UPPER RIGHT SLEEVE

Beginning just above elbow, with MC, ch 58 (60, 66, 72).

ROW 1: Sk first ch from hook (counts as tch here and throughout), sc in next ch, * ch 1, sk 1 st, sc in next ch, rep from * across, turn—58 (60, 66, 72) sts, incl tch.

Work in patt st for 8 (8, 10, 12) rows.

NEXT ROW (INCREASE ROW): Ch 1, sc-flo in next ch, ch 1, sk 1 st, sc-flo in next ch, ch 1, sc-flo in next sc, ch 1, sc-flo in next ch, work in est patt across until 6 sts remain, ch 1, sc-flo in next sc, ch 1, (sc-flo in next ch, ch 1, sk 1 st) twice, sc-flo in tch, turn—62 (64, 70, 76) sts, incl tch.

Work in patt st for 7 rows.

SHAPE UNDERARM

ROW 1: Ch 1, sl st in each of next 4 sts, ch 1, sc-flo in next ch, work in est patt st across until 5 sts remain, turn leaving rem 5 sts unworked—52 (54, 60, 66) sts, incl tch.

ROW 2: Work in patt st.

ROW 3 (DECREASE ROW): Ch 1, (sc-flo in next ch, ch 1, sk 1 st) twice, sc-flo cl (see Special Stitches), work in est patt across until 9 sts remain, ch 1, sk 1 st, sc-flo cl, (ch 1, sk 1 st, sc-flo in next ch) twice, ch 1, sk 1 st, sc-flo in tch, turn—48 (50, 56, 62) sts, incl tch.

ROWS 4–5: Rep Rows 2 and 3—44 (46, 52, 58) sts, incl tch.

Work even in patt st for 2 rows, then repeat Row 3 once more—40 (42, 48, 54) sts, incl tch.

SIZES 38–40 (40–42)" (96.5–101.5 [101.5–106.5]CM) ONLY

Rep Row 3, then Row 2 once (twice)—44 (46) sts, incl tch.

ALL SIZES

Work in patt st for 9 (9, 11, 13) rows.

Fasten off.

UPPER LEFT SLEEVE

Work as for Upper Right Sleeve to end, fasten off MC. Divide for neck front and back: join CC halfway across row and work in patt st for 31 (31, 33, 33) rows for back neck. Fasten off. Join CC to center st where work was divided and work in patt st for 31 (31, 33, 33) rows on the other side for front neck. Fasten off.

These color block pieces will be the neck opening after sewing them to the front and back.

LOWER RIGHT SLEEVE

Beginning at cuff with MC, ch 48 (50, 56, 62).

ROW 1: Sk first ch from hook (counts as tch), sc in next ch, * ch 1, sk 1 st, sc in next ch, rep from * across, turn—48 (50, 56, 62) sts, incl tch.

ROWS 2–11: Work even in patt st.

ROW 12 (INCREASE ROW): Ch 1 (counts as tch), sc-flo in next ch, ch 1, sk 1 st, sc-flo in next ch, ch 1, sc-flo in next sc, ch 1, sc-flo in next ch, work in est patt across until 5 sts remain, ch 1, sc-flo in next sc, ch 1, (sc-flo in next ch, ch 1, sk 1 st) twice, sc-flo in tch, turn—52 (54, 60, 66) sts, incl tch.

ROW 13: Work in patt st.

ROW 14: Ch 2 (counts as tch), hdc-flo in next ch, * ch 1, sk 1 st, hdc-flo in next ch, rep from * ending with hdc-flo in tch, turn.

Work in patt st for 9 (9, 11, 11) rows.

ROWS 15–16: Rep Row 12 and Row 14—55 (57, 63, 69) sts, incl tch.

ROW 17: Work in patt st.

ROW 18: Repeat Row 12 but only work the increase at the beg of row—57 (59, 65, 71) sts, incl tch.

Work in patt st for 11 (13, 15, 17) rows. Rep Row 14 once, then work in patt st for 13 rows.

Fasten off each side.

LOWER LEFT SLEEVE

Work as for Lower Right Sleeve through Row 18. Switch to CC and work as follows:

ROW 1: Ch 1, sc-flo in next ch, * ch 1, sk 1 st, sc-flo in next ch, rep from * ending with sc-flo in tch, turn.

ROWS 2–3: Ch 3, dc-flo in next ch, * ch 1, sk 1 st, dc-flo in next ch, rep from * ending with dc-flo in tch, turn.

Continue in patt st working 2 (2, 3, 3) rows in sc-flo, followed by 3 rows in dc-flo and 1 row in sc-flo.

Switch to MC and work in patt st for 12 (14, 16, 18) rows or until piece measures even with Lower Right Sleeve.

Fasten off.

FINISHING

Weave in ends. Spray block pieces to final dimensions according to the schematic (see Block It sidebar on page 66). Follow the assembly chart on page 50. With yarn needle and RS facing, sew two Back pieces. The seam makes up the center back. With WS facing, sew CC panel of Front Right to the center MC section. With RS together, sew both pieces of Front half sections together at last row worked. The seam makes up center front. With RS together, sew front and back together at side seam. Sew Upper Sleeves to increase sections for underarm seam. For the panel at the neck opening (where you divided the stitches at Upper Sleeve Left), continue sewing to top of front and back and also sew the last row worked to the last row of the Upper Right Sleeve. With RS together, sew Lower Sleeves to ends of Upper Sleeves.

technically speaking: A NOTE ON GAUGE

As you likely already know, gauge refers to the number of stitches and rows in a given area of fabric. Every crochet pattern lists the gauge needed to obtain a finished product in the dimensions listed. You need to crochet to that gauge. That's why most patterns also say that you should "adjust your hook size as necessary." If you crochet too many stitches to an inch in your gauge swatch, you should go up a hook size or two and see if you can get closer to the right gauge. If you crocheted too few stitches to an inch, go down a hook size or two. That's the very basic idea of gauge. But let's go a step beyond that, okay?

Say you have a sweater's worth of gorgeous yarn you've been saving for the perfect pattern and it's DK weight alpaca. Caramel in color, soft as *buttah*. And say you find the perfect pattern. You know it because your heart skipped a beat the first time you saw it. Only thing is, the pattern specifies worsted-weight yarn. Do you put the pattern back, dejected? NO! Take that pattern home.

It just takes a little math to adjust a pattern for a different gauge. It's all about ratios. (Be aware, however, that many patterns are gorgeous in a particular fiber but dreadful in another; it might also happen that the sweater looks very different if you adapt it to a significantly different gauge. Swatch. Swatch often.)

To adjust the pattern, crochet a generous gauge swatch in your perfect yarn. Measure the gauge in the same unit as the pattern. Say the gauge you got is:

4 SC AND 5 ROWS = 1" (2.5 CM)

and say the gauge specified in the pattern is:

3 SC AND 4 ROWS = 1" (2.5 CM)

Since length is usually easier to accommodate than width if shaping and stitch patterns are involved, let's adjust the pattern based on the ratio of stitches. Let's say the pattern says to chain 100 to begin making your size. How many do you chain with your perfect yarn?

$$\frac{4}{3} = \frac{X}{100} \quad \left(\frac{\text{your gauge}}{\text{pattern gauge}} = \frac{X}{\text{original \# of chains}} \right)$$

Cross multiply: 4 x 100 = 400. And 400/3 = 133 (rounded). And there you have it. In order to use your perfect yarn, chain 133 to begin. Do the same simple ratio conversion for all of the stitch counts in the pattern, and you'll be good to go. Remember to keep an eye on your row gauge and adjust as necessary to keep the garment shaped correctly. Also, be sure to account for stitch repeats that require a certain multiple of stitches or rows and adjust accordingly. If it turns out that a larger size in the pattern calls for chaining 133, just follow the instructions for that size.

PHOTO BY BRIAN COSTEDIO

designer in profile

melissa "*missa*" hills

You might know Missa as the Midnight Knitter (midnightknitter .com)—she's been blogging for more than four years. Or maybe you know her from the innumerable buttons and banners she's made for yarny bloggers over the years. Or maybe you've bought yarn from the online shop she runs out of her friend Jessica's barn (in partnership with Jessica, of course), kpixie.com. Missa and Jessica are way fun, doubled-over-laughing fun. You'll hug them after only knowing them for five minutes fun.

Missa loves natural fibers and has a great sense of color and texture. You can envision most of her designs being sported by tortured indie musicians and hardcore rockers alike. Likewise, the yarns she and Jessica stock are luscious and hard to find, and they have become the darlings of urban bloggers all over North America. I'm in love with the sweater she designed for this book, and I think it's fantastic that its deconstruction is a major part of her vision of the garment.

Missa loves horror flicks and Dean Koontz books, and her favorite snack is yogurt with sugar on top. She's done origami since she was eight years old, and she also does modular origami (I admit I have no idea what that is). She knits, makes lip balms from beeswax and oils, sews, makes copper twirling sprinklers, and dabbles in all sorts of other crafty goodness.

Her first published crochet pattern was in the premier issue of CrochetMe.com, although neither of us can remember who found whom. Missa is one of the first CrochetMe.com designers I ever met in person, and so I know for certain that whole bit I wrote about hugging is true.

MISSA IS UP ALL NIGHT ON MIDNIGHTKNITTER.COM

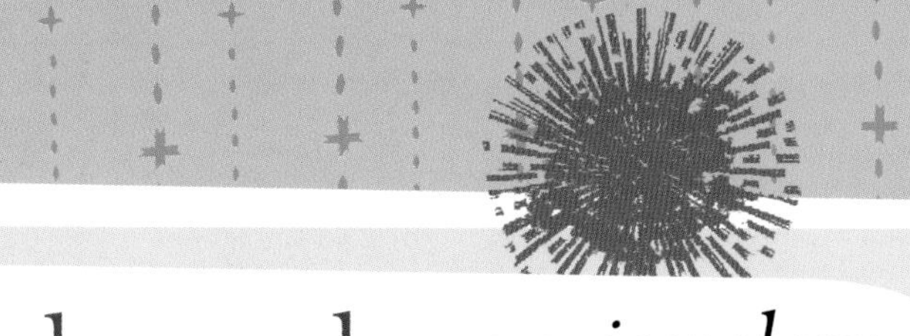

style moderne *jewelery*

Chloe Nightingale

concentration rating 1 **2** 3 4

CHLOE'S INSPIRATION

I've liked the Art Deco style since I was a little kid—the stark blocks of color, the unusual angles, the streamlined shapes, the whole retro-modern shebang. I just can't get enough of it. Even now, when I see a deco building or a lamp, I squeal with delight. With this inspiration in the back of my mind, the idea for this jewelry just popped into my head one day, and I'm so glad it did! I made several coordinating pieces in a variety of sizes from a necklace to a cuff bracelet that can be made larger to be an armband or a choker.

FINISHED SIZE

Necklace: 18" (45.5 cm) circumference and 1½" (3.8 cm) wide at widest point. *Diamond cuff/choker:* 7 (8, 9, 10, 12, 13)" (18 [20.5, 23, 25.5, 30.5, 33] cm) finished circumference and 1½" (3.8 cm) wide at widest point.

YARN

J. & P. Coats Royale Metallic Crochet Thread, Size 10 (88% mercerized cotton, 12% metallic; 100 yds [91 m]/ball): 226G Natural/Gold (MC), 1 ball and 90G Gold/Gold (CC2), 1 ball. Yarn distributed by Coats & Clark.

J. & P. Coats Royale Classic Crochet Thread, Size 10 (100% mercerized cotton; 350 yds [320 m]/ball): 12 Black, (CC1), 1 ball. Yarn distributed by Coats & Clark.

SUBSTITUTION: *Necklace:* About 27 yd (25 m) size 10 cotton crochet thread in MC and 11 yd (10 m) size 10 in each of two colors (CC1 and CC2). *Diamond cuff/choker (all sizes):* About 16 yd (15 m) size 10 cotton crochet thread in MC and 27 yd (25 m) size 10 cotton crochet thread in CC1.

HOOK

Size 8 (1.50 mm) steel hook. Change hook size if necessary to obtain the correct gauge.

NOTIONS

Yarn needle; sewing needle; sewing thread; stitch marker; small button (optional; I use the ⅜–½" [1–1.3 cm] diameter spares that come with dress shirts).

GAUGE

Necklace: 34 sc = 4" (10 cm). *Diamond cuff/choker:* 8 diamonds = 4" (10 cm) (see page 58 for Basic Diamond).

+ SPECIAL STITCHES +

SC2TOG-SK: Single-crochet 2 sts together (decrease), skipping middle st: Insert hook into first st, yo, pull up lp, sk next st, insert hook into next st, yo, pull up lp, yo, pull through all 3 lps on hook.

NECKLACE

With MC, ch 132.

ROW 1: Starting in 2nd ch from hook, sc in each of next 64 chs, sc2tog-sk (see Special Stitches) over next 3 chs, sc in each ch to end, turn—129 sts total.

ROW 2: Ch 1, starting in first sc, sc in each of next 63 sts, sc2tog-sk over next 3 sts, sc in each st to end, fasten off—127 sts total. Turn. With CC1, ch 12, sl st in first ch to form ring, work 16 sc into ring, sl st in first sc to join round.

ROW 3: Without fastening off, sc in the last st worked in Row 2 and in each of next 61 sts, sc2tog-sk over next 3 sts, sc in each st to end—125 sts total.

Without fastening off, ch 8, sl st in first ch to form ring, work 12 sc into ring, sl st in first sc to join round, fasten off. Turn.

ROW 4: With CC2, attach yarn in the last st worked in Row 3, sc in same st and in each st to end.

Fasten off.

TRIANGLE MOTIF

With MC, ch 11.

ROW 1: Starting in 2nd ch from hook, sc in each ch across, turn—10 sts total.

ROW 2: Starting in 2nd st from hook, sc in each st across, turn—9 sts total.

ROWS 3–10: Rep Row 2, decreasing 1 st at the beginning of each row until there is only 1 st rem.

Turn to work along side edge, ch 1, work 1 sc in the end of each row until you reach the foundation chain—10 sts along edge.

Turn to work along foundation chain, ch 3, sc in first ch, sc in each ch across—10 sts along top.

Turn to work along second side edge, ch 3, sc in first ch, work 1 sc in the end of each row for 3 rows, place marker, continue to work sc along edge until you reach the bottom point of the triangle, sc in the ch at the tip, fasten off—10 sts along edge and 1 st at tip.

Working towards the bottom point of the triangle, attach CC1 to the marked stitch, remove marker, ch 2 (counts as 1st dc), dc in next st, hdc in each of next 2 sts, sc in each of next 4 sts, work 3 sc into the sc at the tip of the previous row, sc in each of next 4 sts (you are now working along the other side of the triangle), hdc in each of next 2 sts, dc in each of next 2 sts, turn—19 sts total.

Ch 3 (counts as first dc), dc in next st, hdc in each of next 2 sts, sc in each of next 11 sts, hdc in each of next 2 sts, dc in each of next 2 sts, fasten off—19 sts total.

Attach CC2 in last st worked, sc in same st and in each of next 9 sts, sc in next st, ch 3, sc in first ch (picot made), sc in same st as last sc on triangle and in each st to end.

Fasten off.

DIAMOND CUFF/CHOKER

With CC1, ch 12, sl st in first ch to form ring, work 16 sc into ring, sl st in first sc to join round, do not fasten off. Continue with Basic Diamond.

BASIC DIAMOND

With CC1, ch 5.

ROW 1: Starting in 2nd ch from hook, sc in each ch across, turn—4 sts total.

ROW 2: Ch 1 (does not count as st), sc in each st across, turn—4 sts total.

ROWS 3–4: Repeat Row 2.

Without fastening off, continue to repeat the basic diamond, forming a chain of diamonds, until you have a total of 11 (13, 15, 17, 21, 23) diamonds.

Without fastening off, ch 8, sl st in first ch to form ring, work 12 sc into ring, sl st in first sc to join round, fasten off.

EDGING

ROW 1: Attach MC to top point of far right-end diamond (you will be repeating this on the other side and the bracelet is symmetrical so do not be worried about which side is the top), ch 1, sc in same st, * ch 4, sc in tip of next diamond; rep from * across, turn—51 (61, 71, 81, 101, 111) sts total.

ROW 2: Ch 1, sc in each st across, fasten off. Turn.

ROW 3: Attach CC1 to last st worked, ch 3 (counts as first dc, ch 1), sk next st, dc in next st, *ch 1, sk next st, dc in next st; rep from * 10 (12, 14, 16, 20, 22) more times, fasten off—25 (29, 35, 39, 49, 55) sts total. Turn.

ROW 4: Attach MC to last st worked, ch 1, sc in same st, *work sc into ch-1 sp, sc in top of next dc; rep from * across, ending sc in last ch-1 (corner) sp, sc in second st of beg ch-3, fasten off. Turn.

Rotate work 180° (do not flip). Repeat Rows 1–4 for other side.

Fasten off.

FINISHING

Weave in ends. Block all pieces (see Block It sidebar on page 66). Attach triangle motif to point of necklace by sewing it with a needle and thread. If you sew carefully between the back bumps (from the sts) of the motif to the front bumps (bits of the stitches) of the necklace and use matching thread, your stitches will not be noticeable.

To fasten the jewelry, you have two options: The easiest way is to stuff or button the bigger-loop end into the smaller-loop end. The other option is to sew a small button onto the smaller loop (or just omit the smaller loop when making the necklace and sew the button directly on the end) and button it into the bigger loop.

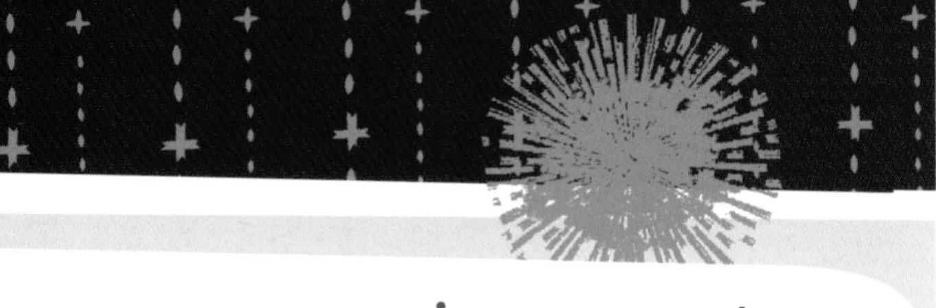

mesmerize *sweater*

Kristin Omdahl

concentration rating 1 2 3 4

KRISTIN'S INSPIRATION

I wanted a design that incorporated swirling motifs into a sweater that had no structured, conventional pieces, and no beginning or end. I made the small motifs first and pinned them to my dress form in various positions before I decided where and how to use them. Then I added to the motifs in different directions to create shapes to drape the dress form. What emerged was a sweater-shaped pattern with flowing kimono sleeves and side vents. All stitches are worked in the back loop only. I used the accent yarn to reverse single crochet in the remaining loop. The resulting piping texture blends all the pieces together as if the entire garment were made in one piece.

FINISHED SIZE

BUST CIRCUMFERENCE: 36 (40, 44, 48)" (91.5 [101.5, 112, 122] cm) to fit bust sizes 32 (36, 40, 44)" (86.5 [91.5, 101.5, 112] cm).

YARN

Tilli Tomas Pure & Simple (100% silk, 260 yd [238 m]/100 g): gloxinia (MC), 5 (6, 7, 8) skeins.

Tilli Tomas Disco Lights (90% spun silk, 10% petite sequins, 225 yd [206 m]/100 g): gloxinia (CC), 2 (3, 3, 3) skeins.

SUBSTITUTION: About 1,300 (1,495, 1,719, 1,977 yd (1,189 [1,367, 1,572, 1,808] m) for MC in DK weight (Light #3) yarn. About 450 (517, 595, 684) yd (411 [473, 544, 625] m) for CC in DK weight (Light #3) yarn.

HOOK

Size G/6 (4.0 mm). Change hook size if necessary to obtain the correct gauge.

NOTIONS

Yarn needle; scissors.

GAUGE

12 dtr stitches and 3 rows of dtr = 4" (10 cm) after blocking.

Note: Gauge is determined *after* blocking, so block your gauge swatch before beginning the pattern. (See Block It sidebar on page 66.)

+ SPECIAL STITCHES +

All stitches are worked through back loop only unless otherwise noted.

HDC-BLO: Work hdc through the back lp only.

HDC2TOG-BLO: [Yo, insert hook through back lp of next st and pull up a lp] twice (5 lps on hook), yo and pull through all 5 lps (decrease made).

DC-BLO: Work dc through the back lp only.

DC2TOG-BLO: [Yo, insert hook through back lp of next st and pull up a lp, yo and pull through 2 lps] twice (3 lps on hook), yo and pull through all 3 lps (decrease made).

REVERSE SINGLE CROCHET (REV SC): Working left to right, insert hook in first st to the right, complete as for sc (lefties work right to left).

TR-BLO: Work a tr through the back lp only.

DTR-BLO: Work a double treble crochet through the back lp only.

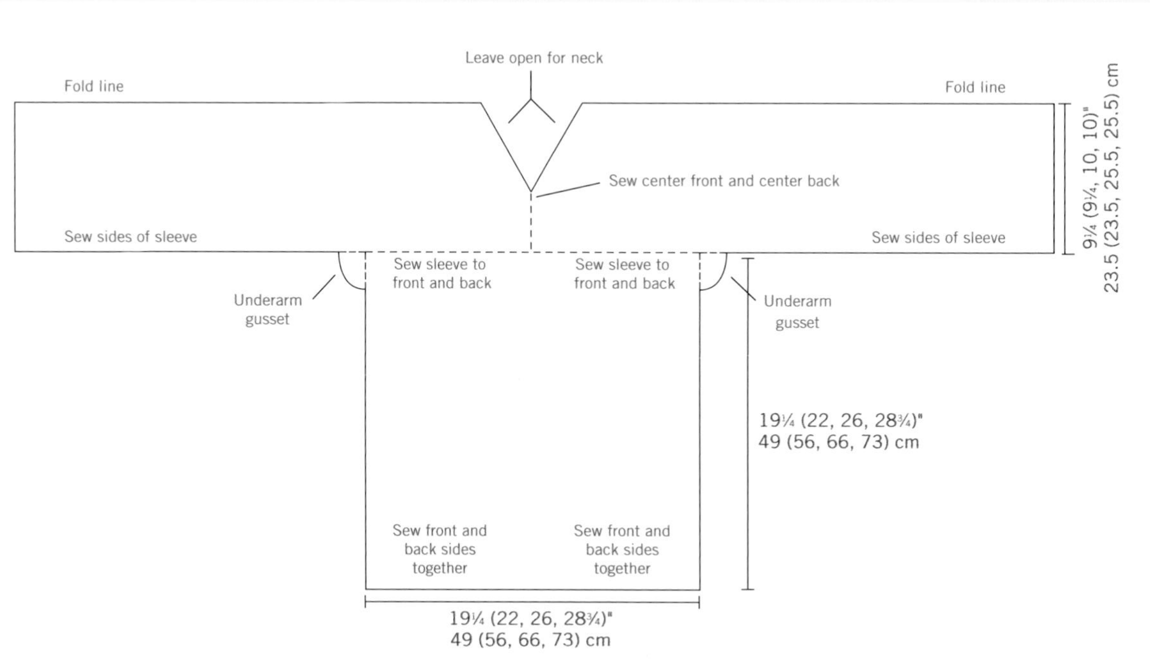

MOTIF
(Make 4)

With MC, ch 4, sl st in first ch to form ring.

RND 1: Ch 1, work 8 sc into ring, do not join, place marker in first st to mark beginning of round, move marker up with each new round—8 sts.

Note: After Rnd 1, rounds are worked in a spiral without joining.

RND 2: [2 hdc-blo in next st] 5 times, [2 dc-blo in next st] 3 times—16 sts. (See Special Stitches.)

RND 3: [2 dc–blo in next st] 6 times, [2 tr-blo in next st] 7 times, tr-blo in next st, 2 tr-blo in next st, tr-blo in next st—30 sts. (See Special Stitches.)

RND 4: [2 tr-blo in next st, tr-blo in next st] 5 times, [2 tr-blo in next st] 3 times, tr-blo in next st, [2 tr-blo in next st] 2 times—40 sts.

RND 5: [2 tr-blo in next st, tr-blo in each of next 4 sts] 8 times—48 sts.

RND 6: [2 dtr-blo in next st, dtr-blo in each of next 5 sts] 8 times—56 sts. (See Special Stitches.)

Work tr-blo in next st, dc-blo in next st, hdc-blo in next st, sc-blo in next st, sl st-blo in next st. Fasten off.

With sl st join CC in free lp (unworked front loop) of last stitch worked, ch 1, sc in same st, rev sc in free lp of each st worked, all the way back to the beginning of the spiral. Fasten off. Pull tail through original ch-4 lp and fasten to wrong side.

LOWER FRONT AND BACK
(Make 2)

Note: Continuation of motif is worked in rows, so be careful to work through the back loops only (blo) on the right side and through the front loops only (flo) on the wrong side. You might find it helpful to mark the right side with a stitch marker to avoid confusion.

ROW 1 (RS): Ch 5 (counts as first dtr here and throughout), dtr-blo in same st, dtr-blo in each of next 4 sts, [2 dtr-blo in next st, dtr-blo in each of next 4 sts] 5 times, turn—36 sts.

ROW 2: Ch 5, dtr-flo in same st, dtr-flo in each of next 5 sts, [2 dtr-flo in next st, dtr-flo in each of next 5 sts] 5 times, turn—42 sts.

ROW 3: Ch 5, dtr-blo in same st, dtr-blo in each of next 6 sts, [2 dtr-blo in next st, dtr-blo in each of next 6 sts] 5 times, turn—48 sts.

ROWS 4–10: Continue to increase each row as established, working one additional dtr st between increases until there are 13 dtr between increases—90 sts.

SIZE 40" (101.5 CM) ONLY

ROWS 11–12: Continue to increase as established, working one additional dtr st between increases until there are 15 dtr between increases—102 sts.

SIZE 44" (112 CM) ONLY

ROWS 11–15: Continue to increase as established, working one additional dtr st between increases until there are 18 dtr between increases—120 sts.

SIZE 48" (122 CM) ONLY

ROWS 11–17: Continue to increase as established, working one additional dtr st between increases until there are 20 dtr between increases—132 sts.

Fasten off MC. With sl st join CC in free lp of last stitch worked with sl st, ch 1, sc in same st, rev sc into free lp of each stitch worked all the way back to the beginning of the motif.

Note: Every free loop created with MC will be covered with a rev sc with CC. Although this step could be worked after assembly, it is easier to manipulate the pieces (i.e., front, back, sleeves) before seaming.

BODICE AND SLEEVE

(Make 2)

RND 1: Working through blo, join MC to any stitch of a motif, ch 5 (counts as first dtr), dtr-blo in same stitch, dtr-blo in each of next 6 sts, * 2 dtr-blo in next st, dtr-blo in each of next 6 sts, rep from * around—64 sts.

RND 2: Ch 5, dtr-blo in same st, dtr-blo in each of next 7 sts, * 2 dtr-blo in next st, dtr-blo in each of next 7 sts, rep from * around—72 sts.

RND 3: Ch 5, dtr-blo in same st, dtr-blo in each of next 8 sts, * 2 dtr-blo in next st, dtr-blo in each of next 8 sts, rep from * around—80 sts.

RND 4: Ch 5, dtr-blo in same st, dtr-blo in each of next 9 sts, * 2 dtr-blo in next st, dtr-blo in each of next 9 sts, rep from * around—88 sts.

RND 5: Ch 5, dtr-blo in same st, dtr-blo in each of next 10 sts, * 2 dtr-blo in next st, dtr-blo in each of next 10 sts, rep from * around—96 sts.

SIZES 44 (48)" (112 [122]CM) ONLY

Work one more increase row as established, adding one additional dtr-blo between increases—104 sts.

Note: Remainder of sleeve is worked in rows, so be careful to work through the back loops only (blo) on the right side, and through the front loops only (flo) on the wrong side. Mark the right side with a stitch marker to avoid confusion.

ROW 6 (RS): Ch 5, dtr-blo in same st, dtr-blo in each of next 5 sts, * 2 dtr-blo in next st, dtr-blo in each of next 5 sts, rep from * 7 times, dtr-blo in each of next 0 (0, 4, 4) sts, turn—56 (56, 60, 60) sts.

ROW 7: Ch 5, dtr-flo in each st across, turn—56 (56, 60, 60) sts.

ROW 8–9: Rep Row 7 two more times, alternating blo for RS and flo for WS.

Turn sleeve around to work rows on the other half of Motif that has thus far only been worked in rounds. Repeat Rows 6–9. Then repeat Row 7 three more times.

With sl st join CC in free lp of last st worked, ch 1, sc in same st, rev sc in free lp of each st worked all the way back to the beginning of the motif.

FINISHING

Wet-block each piece (see Block It sidebar on page 66) and pin to dimensions according to the schematic. Let dry.

With yarn needle, sew "bodice section" of sleeves to top of lower body, centering the joining of right and left sleeves to the center front and center back, using the diagram on page 62 as a guide. Sew the side seams of the Lower Front and Back, starting 2–3" (5–7.5 cm) from the top (see Undersleeve Gusset below) and stopping 6" (15 cm) from the bottom (side vents). Sew sleeve seams, starting at the sleeve cuff end of last row, and stopping 2–3" from the top (see Undersleeve Gusset below).

UNDERSLEEVE GUSSET

To facilitate ease in movement, kimono sleeves require an undersleeve gusset. Leaving a 2–3" (5–7.5 cm) unsewn edge at the top of each side and inside of each sleeve center will give you a somewhat circular opening of about 4–6" (10–15 cm) in diameter at the underarm. See the assembly diagram on page 62 for approximate location of gusset.

With the following instructions, you will be working a circular gusset directly into the stitches surrounding this opening:

With MC, work 1 dc in each st around and 4 dtr into the end of each dtr row around. On next round, work dc2tog-blo (see Special Stitches) around. On next round, work hdc-blo (see Special Stitches) into each st around. On next round, work hdc2tog-blo (see Special Stitches) around. On next round, work hdc-blo around. Fasten off. With tapestry needle, weave tail through all sts remaining, pull tightly and fasten off. Pull to wrong side and weave in tail. Repeat for second side.

technically speaking: BLOCK IT! JUST BLOCK IT!

Blocking is the closest thing to magic you'll find in crochet. In fact, it pretty much *is* magic, without any pesky incantations to remember. Blocking is what you do to crocheted fabric to make it behave nicely, drape beautifully, and otherwise be all it can be. You also block finished pieces after you wash them so they go back to being lovely when they dry. Regardless of which method you choose, be sure to treat animal fibers (wools, alpaca, and mohair) carefully so they don't felt. Don't agitate the fibers, don't use hot water or harsh detergents, and don't switch rapidly from one water temperature to another. Keep synthetics away from high heat. There are three general techniques for blocking crocheted fabric:

1. **SPRAY BLOCKING:** Pin the pieces or the finished garment to the specified dimensions. Use clean carpet, a mattress, or a schmancy blocking board as a surface, and always use rust-proof pins. Spray the pieces evenly using a spray bottle and tepid water. Let dry. Remove the pins and voilà: The piece retains its blocked shape. This method is great for all natural fibers, but it might have little effect on synthetics. You can also block the edges of lace shawls so they stay nice and pointy, wavy, or flat. Don't be afraid to use an enormous number of pins.

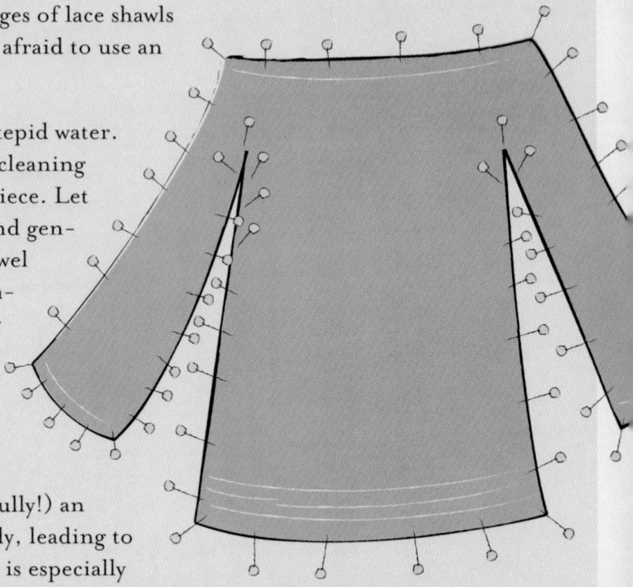

2. **WET BLOCKING:** Gently submerge the fabric in tepid water. Again, be very careful with animal fibers. If you're cleaning the piece, use a mild wool wash. Don't agitate the piece. Let it soak for fifteen minutes or so. Drain the water and gently squeeze out the excess. Lay the piece on a dry towel and gently roll the towel over it to get even more water out. Pin the piece as directed for spray blocking above or for a garment, lay it on a flat surface. Let it dry. This method is also good for natural fibers and for delicate synthetics that shouldn't be machine washed.

3. **STEAM BLOCKING:** Use a steamer or (very carefully!) an iron's steam. The steam relaxes the fibers beautifully, leading to maximum sheen and stunning drape. This method is especially magical on silk and synthetic fibers—you'll be shocked by how even the roughest acrylics can drape after being steam blocked. But be very careful when steam blocking synthetics, as many of them can be ruined by excessive heat. Always err on the side of caution, and hold the steam about 10" (25 cm) from the fabric. Some natural fibers are also very heat sensitive. Always read yarn labels carefully for care information.

designer in profile

kristin omdahl

PHOTO BY JOHN THAWLEY

Kristin is a force of nature. One moment no-nonsense and all business, the next proclaiming the awesomeness of a deep-fried delicacy with a funny name at a decades-old restaurant in her hometown, Detroit. To call her prolific would be an understatement. She produces, in the time it would take me to design and crochet a 6" (15 cm) doll, an original, enormous, intricate lace shawl. Then she sells or self-publishes the pattern and moves on to the next of a dozen projects. She moves quickly when she knits as well and often duplicates a crochet design in knit fabric to exploit the qualities of both crafts.

Kristin was living abroad when she was pregnant with her now five-year-old son. Overcome by a desire to crochet booties, she battled a language barrier, paltry yarn options, and overseas shipping to learn the craft. Whereas many of us would stare at a misshapen bootie it took five hours to produce and put down the hook forever, Kristin stared at her first misshapen bootie and felt empowered. She went on to make multiple layettes, and after her son was born, moved on to designing her own shawls and garments. Passionate about math, her designs often feature intricate geometric elements and true elegance in shaping.

Although she sold one-of-a-kind garments to boutiques for several years, she didn't identify herself as a designer. "If asked what I did for a living," she says, "I would give a long, awkward description of how I knitted and crocheted and made garments and sold them individually. I was documenting my patterns for about a year before I thought to sell the patterns themselves. When I starting getting paid for design work and publication, I felt comfortable calling myself a designer."

VISIT KRISTIN AT STYLEDBYKRISTIN.COM.

shades of plaid *scarves*

Julie Armstrong Holetz

concentration rating 1 2 3 4

JULIE'S INSPIRATION

I have an experimental, research-based personality. When I get an idea in my head I have to test it, record it, and photograph it. One day I had the idea of crocheting a plaid design and felting it. There are several ways to go plaid with crochet: surface stitching, complicated color changes, and woven mesh. I settled on a mesh pattern with a woven chain. I photographed my swatch before and after felting. I hated the felted version, so I ditched it. Then, a friend saw the before photo and said it would make a great scarf. She was right! Voilà, a design was born.

FINISHED SIZE

5½" (14 cm) wide and 62" (157.5 cm) long, excluding fringe.

YARN

Blue scarf: Cascade 220 (100% wool, 220 yd [201 m]/100 g): #9420 blue, 1 skein (MC); #7822 brown, 1 skein (CC1); #2415 tan, 1 skein (CC2). *Pink scarf (page 70):* Cascade 220 (100% wool, 220 yd [201 m]/100 g): #9478 pink, 1 skein (MC); #7814 green, 1 skein (CC1); #2415 tan, 1 skein (CC2).

SUBSTITUTION: About 500 yd (457 m) worsted-weight (Medium #4) wool.

HOOK

Size J/10 (6 mm) and K/10½ (6.5 mm). Change hook size if necessary to obtain the correct gauge.

NOTIONS

Yarn needle.

GAUGE

For gauge swatch, work first 9 rows of Mesh Panel (page 70). 8 sts and 7 rows = 4" (10 cm) with smaller hook in mesh stripe pattern.

+ SPECIAL STITCHES +

MESH STRIPE PATTERN

ROWS 1–4: In MC.

ROWS 5–6: In CC1.

ROWS 7–10: In MC.

ROWS 11–14: In CC2.

Rep Rows 1–14 for Stripe Patt.

CHAIN WEAVE SEQUENCE

ROWS 1–3: CC1.

ROWS 4–6: MC.

ROWS 7–8: CC2.

ROWS 9–10: MC.

MESH PANEL

With smaller hook and MC, ch 22.

ROW 1: Skip first 3 ch (count as hdc, ch 1), hdc in next ch, *ch 1, sk 1 ch, hdc in next ch; rep from * to end, turn—10 ch-1 sps.

ROW 2: Ch 3 (counts as hdc, ch 1), sk first 2 sts, *hdc in next st, ch 1, sk 1 st; rep from * across, hdc in 2nd ch of beg ch-3, turn.

Working in mesh stripe pattern (see Special Stitches), rep Row 2 for 62" (157.5 cm).

Fasten off.

WEAVING CHAINS

With larger hook, MC and leaving a 7" (18 cm) tail at the beginning and end of each chain, ch 200. Fasten off. Make a total of 5 chains in MC, 3 chains in CC1, and 2 chains in CC2.

FINISHING

Weave in ends on mesh panel. Thread tail end of one CC1 chain onto yarn needle. Beginning at one side of the scarf and working lengthwise, weave length of chain loosely in and out of ch-1 spaces of the Mesh Panel. Follow chain weave sequence (see Special Stitches) and work each chain beginning in the same direction as the first.

ADD FRINGE

Cut 30 lengths of MC, 18 lengths of CC1, and 12 lengths of CC2, each 14" (35.5 cm) long. Using 3 strands at a time, thread one end of the fringe into ch-1 sp of the same color. Gather the tail end of the weaving chain and tie all ends together with an overhand knot to secure fringe. Follow woven chains for placement of fringe on each side of the scarf. Trim fringe.

technically speaking: CROCHET SAMPLER

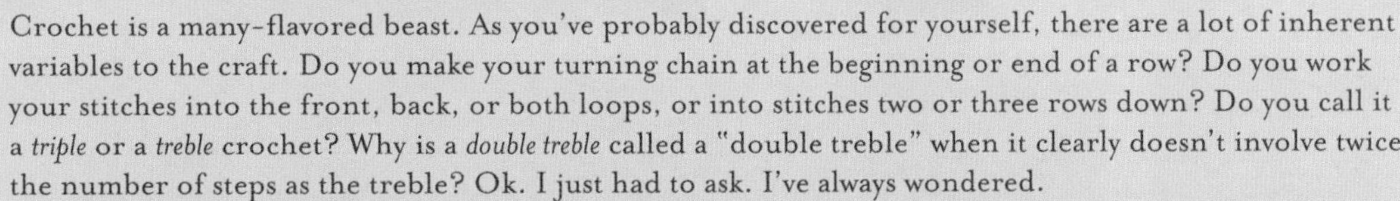

Crochet is a many-flavored beast. As you've probably discovered for yourself, there are a lot of inherent variables to the craft. Do you make your turning chain at the beginning or end of a row? Do you work your stitches into the front, back, or both loops, or into stitches two or three rows down? Do you call it a *triple* or a *treble* crochet? Why is a *double treble* called a "double treble" when it clearly doesn't involve twice the number of steps as the treble? Ok. I just had to ask. I've always wondered.

Beyond these variables that each affect the way your work turns out, there are many different types of crochet, some which deviate profoundly from basic crochet techniques. Here's a sampler:

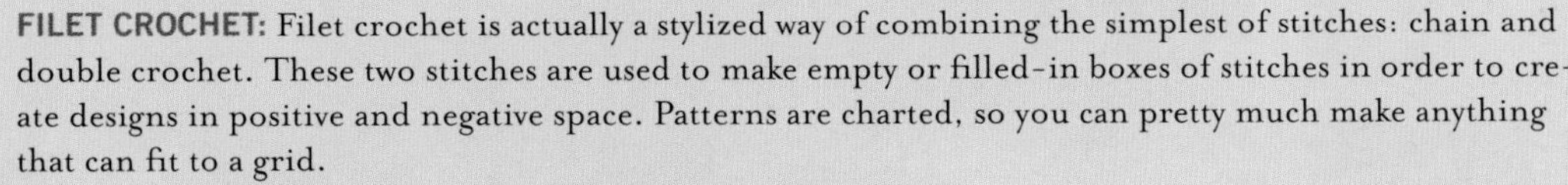

FILET CROCHET: Filet crochet is actually a stylized way of combining the simplest of stitches: chain and double crochet. These two stitches are used to make empty or filled-in boxes of stitches in order to create designs in positive and negative space. Patterns are charted, so you can pretty much make anything that can fit to a grid.

TAPESTRY CROCHET: This is also a type of basic crochet that involves a special way of making single crochet stitches to work graphical patterns in two or more colors. You carry the unused color along with the working color by laying the yarn over the stitches as you work them, thus hiding the unused color in the body of your stitching. This creates a dense fabric. To experience it for yourself check out the felted Variations Baskets by Carol Ventura and related technique sidebar starting on page 118.

TUNISIAN CROCHET (AKA AFGHAN CROCHET): Ok, this one is totally different from the basics. A big long (14" [35.5 cm]) crochet hook is used for this type of crochet. You use it to pick up a loop in each stitch across a row, then you work back across the row binding off those stitches. The fabric created has a very different texture from normal crocheted fabric. You should try it. Check out Megan Granholm's Five O'Clock Tank and related Tunisian crochet technique sidebar starting on page 98.

HAIRPIN LACE: Now, this technique is sort of a hybrid. Hairpin lace requires a special hairpin tool that consists of two posts. You wrap yarn around the posts and work single crochet stitches up the middle. This is very difficult to explain in just words. Check out Jennifer Hansen of StitchDiva.com for tutorials and cool patterns using hairpin lace.

IRISH CROCHET: Ok, we're back to the basic stitches again. Irish crochet is a particular tradition of lace crochet worked with very lightweight thread and a tiny steel hook, involving making 3-D motifs and placing them against a mesh background. It's absolutely breathtaking. Check out Annette Petavy's take on a contemporary Irish crochet shawl at CrochetMe.com/irish-oranges.

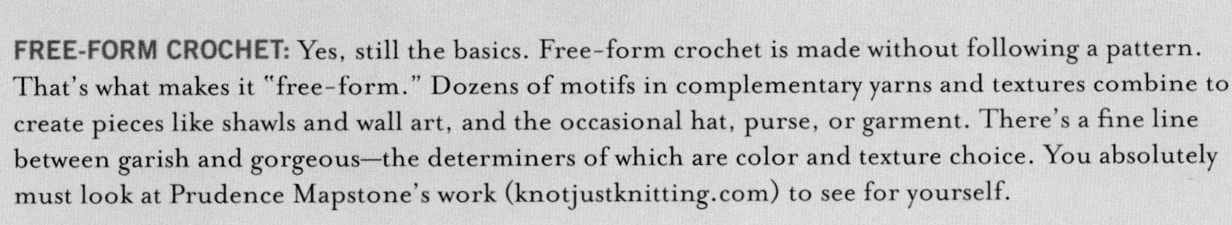

FREE-FORM CROCHET: Yes, still the basics. Free-form crochet is made without following a pattern. That's what makes it "free-form." Dozens of motifs in complementary yarns and textures combine to create pieces like shawls and wall art, and the occasional hat, purse, or garment. There's a fine line between garish and gorgeous—the determiners of which are color and texture choice. You absolutely must look at Prudence Mapstone's work (knotjustknitting.com) to see for yourself.

leaves *sweater*

Annette Petavy

concentration rating 1 2 3 **4**

ANNETTE'S INSPIRATION

This garment is a dream. Inspired by nature's mysteries, it's a dream about a life closer to nature, filled with more poetry than daily grind. A life in which you have the time to play and listen to the wind blowing through the trees. The seed beads bordering the leaves are reminiscent of dewdrops glistening in the morning sun, and they also give this sweater an elegant drape.

FINISHED SIZE

BUST CIRCUMFERENCE: 34 (37½, 41, 44½)" (86.5 [95, 104, 112.5] cm). To fit chest size 32½ (36, 39½, 43)" (82.5 [91.5, 100.5, 109] cm).

YARN

Jaeger Matchmaker Merino 4 ply (100% wool, 200 yd [183 m]/50 g): #741 Mineral, 7 (7, 9, 10) skeins. Yarn distributed by Westminster Fibers.

SUBSTITUTION: About 1,422 (1,422, 1,750, 1,969) yd (1,300 [1,300, 1,600, 1,800] m) fingering-weight (Fine #2) wool or wool blend.

HOOK

Size G/6 (4 mm). Change hook size if necessary to obtain the correct gauge.

NOTIONS

Yarn needle; sewing needle; matching sewing thread; about 1,400 (1,600, 1,700, 1,900) seed beads: color crystal, silver lined.

GAUGE

17 dc and 10.5 rows = 4" (10 cm) in dc.

+ SPECIAL STITCHES +

SHELL: (2 dc, ch 1, 2 dc) all in same space.

LACE PANEL
(see diagram at right)

ROW 1: Into the starting chain, ch 1, sk 1 ch, dc in next ch, sk 2 ch, shell (see above) in next ch, sk 2 ch, dc in next ch, ch 1, sk 1 ch.

ROW 2: Into lace panel from previous row, ch 1, sk ch-1, dc in next st, sk 2 dc, shell in next ch-1 sp, sk 2 dc, dc in next st, ch 1, sk ch-1.

TRANSITIONING LACE PANELS INTO PLAIN STITCHES
(see diagram at right)

To allow for smooth shaping and seamable edges, it is sometimes necessary to transition the lace panel described above into plain double crochets. To maintain gauge, each lace panel is transitioned into 7 dcs. The transition is worked over two rows, as follows:

ROW 1: Dc in ch-1 sp, dc in each of next 2 sts, yo, insert hook in 2nd dc of shell, yo and pull up a lp (3 lps on hook), sk ch-1 sp, yo, insert hook in 3rd dc of shell, yo and pull up a lp (5 lps on hook), yo and pull through all lps on hook, dc in each of next 2 sts, dc in ch-1 sp—7 dc total.

ROW 2: Dc in each st from previous row.

+ PATTERN NOTES +

- When shaping the armholes, sleeve caps and neck, the stitches worked as slip stitches in the beginning of a row or skipped at the end of a row are decreases and are not to be worked in following rows.
- Place a stitch marker in the first stitch (other than a slip stitch) of the row, to facilitate the counting of stitches.
- In the main parts of the garment—back, front and sleeves—the turning chain does not count as a stitch. It will be hidden in the seam. When working the leaves at the bottom of the garment, the turning chain does count as a stitch.

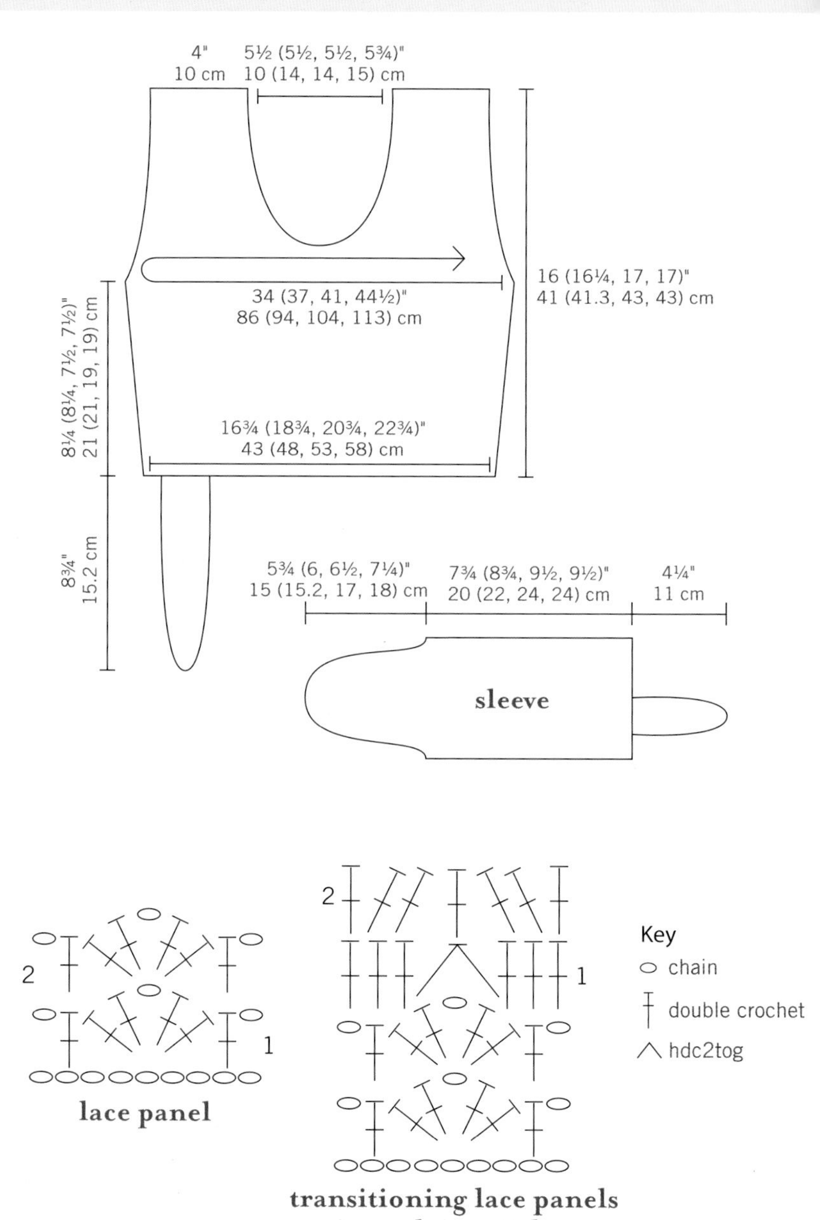

- The garment is composed of vertical dc panels, separated by lace panels.

SWEATER

BACK

Ch 71 (80, 88, 97).

ROW 1: Ch 3 (tch, does not count as a stitch here and throughout), working into both lps dc in each of next 14 (10, 14, 10) ch, *lace panel over next 9 ch, dc in each of next 8 ch; repeat from * 1 (2, 2, 3) more times, work lace panel over next 9 ch, dc in each of last 14 (10, 14, 10) ch, turn.

ROW 2: Ch 3, work in est stitch pattern.

Repeat Row 2. *At the same time,* work bust increases as follows:

BUST INCREASES

The bust increases are worked inside the dc panels. No increases are made in the side panels (the 14 (10, 14, 10) sts at each side of the piece. In each of the other dc panels, one stitch is increased in the center stitch, or the first of the two center stitches if the panel has an even number of stitches. Increase: 2 dc in 1 dc from the previous row (1 st increased).

Start bust increases on Row 3 (3, 3, 5). Increase as described above every 2nd (4th, 4th, 4th) row for a total number of 5 (3, 3, 2) times. When the increases are completed, each dc panel, except the side panels, is composed of 13 (11, 11, 10) dcs.

Work straight until the piece measures 8¼" (8¼, 7½, 7½) (21 [21, 19, 19] cm).

SHAPE ARMHOLES

ROW 1: Sl st in each of first 3 (3, 3, 5) sts, sc in next st, hdc in next st, work across row in est patt until 5 (5, 5, 7) sts remain, hdc in next st, sc in next st, turn leaving rem sts unworked.

SIZE 34" (86.5 CM) ONLY

ROW 2: Sl st in each of first 2 sts, sc in next st, work across row in est patt until 3 sts remain, sc in next st, turn leaving rem sts unworked.

ROW 3: Sl st in first st, sc in next st, work across row in est patt until 2 sts remain, sc in next st, turn leaving rem st unworked.

ROWS 4–6: Ch 3, dc2tog over next 2 sts, work across row in est patt until 2 sts remain, dc2tog over next 2 sts, turn.

Continue working even in est patt until work measures 15¼" (38.5 cm).

SIZES 41 (44½)" (104 [112.5] CM) ONLY

ROW 2: Sl st in each of first 3 sts, ch 3, dc2tog over next 2 sts, work across row in est patt until 5 sts remain, dc2tog over next 2 sts, turn leaving rem sts unworked.

ROWS 3–4: Ch 3, dc2tog over first 2 sts, work across row in est patt until 2 sts remain dc2tog over last 2 sts, turn.

SIZE 37½" (95 CM) ONLY

ROW 5: (The first and last lace panel will be partially transitioned into dc stitches. See Special Stitches.) Ch 3, dc in first st, dc in ch-1 sp, dc in each of next 2 sts, *yo, insert hook in 2nd dc of lace shell, yo and pull up a lp (3 lps on hook), sk ch-1 sp, yo, insert hook in 3rd dc of lace shell, yo and pull up a lp (5 lps on hook), yo and pull through all lps on hook, dc in each of next 2 sts*, ch 1, sk ch-1 sp, dc in next st, work across row in est patt to last lace panel, ch 1, sk ch-1 sp, dc in each of next 2 sts, repeat from * to * across, dc in ch-1 sp, dc in last st, turn.

ROW 6: Ch 3, dc2tog over first 2 sts, dc in each of next 5 sts, ch 1, sk ch-1 sp, work across row in est patt until 8 sts remain, ch 1, sk ch-1 sp, dc in each of next 5 sts, dc2tog over last 2 sts, turn.

ROWS 7–8: Work even in new est patt.

ROW 9: Ch 3, dc2tog over first 2 sts, work across row in est patt until 2 sts remain, dc2tog over last 2 sts, turn.

Work even until piece measures 15½" (39.5 cm).

SIZE 41" (104 CM) ONLY

ROW 5: Work even in est patt.

ROW 6: Ch 3, dc2tog over first 2 sts, work across row in est patt until 2 sts remain, dc-2tog over last 2 sts, turn.

ROWS 7–8: Work even in est patt.

ROW 9: Rep Row 6.

Work even until piece measures 15¾" (40 cms).

SIZE 44½" (112.5 CM) ONLY

ROW 2: Sl st in each of first 3 sts, sc in next st, hdc in next st. Transition the first lace panel into plain stitches (see Special Stitches). Work across row in est patt to last lace panel. Transition last lace panel into plain stitches. Hdc in next st, sc in next st, turn leaving rem sts unworked.

ROW 3: Sl st in each of first 2 sts, ch 3, dc2tog over next 2 sts, dc in each of next 5 sts, work across row in new est patt until 9 sts remain, dc in next 5 sts, dc2tog over next 2 sts, turn leaving rem sts unworked.

ROWS 4–5: Ch 3, dc2tog over first 2 sts, work across row in est patt until 2 sts remain, dc-2tog over last 2 sts, turn.

ROW 6: Work even in est patt.

ROW 7: Rep Row 4.

ROWS 8–9: Work even in est patt.

ROW 10: Rep Row 4.

Work even until piece measures 15¾" (40 cm).

ALL SIZES

Work two rows even, transitioning all remaining lace panels into plain stitches.

SHAPE SHOULDER AND NECK

SIZES 34 (37½)" (86.5 [95] CM) ONLY

ROW 1: Sl st in each of first 2 (3) sts, sc in each of next 2 sts, hdc in next st, dc in each of next 11 sts, {shape for neck over center 25 sts: dc in each of next 3 sts, hdc in each of next 2 sts, sc in each of next 3 sts, sl st in each of next 9 sts, sc in each of next 3 sts, hdc in each of next 2 sts, dc in each of next 3 sts}, dc in each of next 11 sts, hdc in next st, sc in each of next 2 sts, turn leaving rem sts unworked.

ROW 2: Sl st in each of first 7 sts, sc in each of next 2 sts, hdc in each of next 2 sts, dc in each of next 3 sts, sc in next st, fasten off, sk center 23 sts, attach yarn with a sc in next st, dc in each of next 3 sts, hdc in each of next 2 sts, sc in each of next 2 sts. Fasten off.

SIZES 41 (44½)" (105 [113] CM) ONLY

ROW 1: Sl st in each of first 3 sts, sc in next st, hdc in next 1 (2) sts, dc in each st across row until 5 (6) sts remain, hdc in next 1 (2) sts, sc in next st, turn leaving rem sts unworked.

ROW 2: Sl st in each of first 6 sts, sc in next st, hdc in next st, dc in each of next 9 sts, dc in each of next 2 sts, hdc in next st, sc in each of next 2 sts, sl st in each of next 15 (17) sts, sc in each of next 2 sts, hdc in next st, dc in each of next 2 sts, dc in each of next 9 sts, hdc in next st, sc in next st, turn leaving rem sts unworked.

ROW 3: Sl st in each of first 6 sts, sc in each of next 2 sts, hdc in next st, dc in each of next 2 sts, sc in next st, fasten off, sk 23 (25) sts, reattach yarn with sc in next st, dc in each of next 2 sts, hdc in next st, sc in each of next 2 sts. Fasten off.

BACK LEAVES

The leaves are worked from the waist down at the bottom of the back. Turn the work and work Row 1 into the remaining loop of the base chain. All leaves are worked at the same time for first 10 rows. On the following rows, each leaf is worked separately. Please note that there is a side leaf at each side of the garment. The outer edge of the side leaves is worked differently in sizes 34 (41)" (86.5 [104] cm), where the side panel of the back consists of 14

stitches, as compared to sizes 37½ (44½)" (95 [112.5] cm), where the side panel consists of 10 stitches. All other leaves (called "complete leaves") are identical.

ROW 1: Sk first 2 ch. Attach yarn with a dc in 3rd ch, ch 1 (0, 1, 0), sk next 1 (0, 1, 0) ch, dc in next 1 (0, 1, 0) ch, ch 1 (0, 1, 0), sk next 1 (0, 1, 0) ch, dc in next ch, *ch 10, sk 4 ch, dc in each of next 2 sts, work lace panel over next 9 sts (symmetrical to lace panel already worked on back), dc in each of next 2 sts; repeat from * 2 (3, 3, 4) times, ch 10, sk 4 ch, dc in each of next 2 sts, ch 1 (0, 1, 0), sk next 1 (0, 1, 0) ch, dc in next 1 (0, 1, 0) ch, ch 1 (0, 1, 0), sk next 1 (0, 1, 0) ch, dc in next ch, turn.

ROW 2: Ch 3 (counts as dc), sk first st, ch 1 (0, 1, 0), sk next 1 (0, 1, 0) ch, dc in next 1 (0, 1, 0) st, ch 1 (0, 1, 0), sk next 1 (0, 1, 0) ch, dc in next stitch, *ch 10, sk chains from previous row, dc in each of next 2 sts, work lace panel over lace panel from previous row, dc in each of next 2 sts; repeat from * 2 (3, 3, 4) times, ch 10, sk 4 ch, dc in each of next 2 sts, ch 1 (0, 1, 0), sk next 1 (0, 1, 0) ch, dc in next 1 (0, 1, 0) st, ch 1 (0, 1, 0), sk next 1 (0, 1, 0) ch, dc in next stitch, turn.

The basic pattern for the side leaves and the 3 (4, 4, 5) complete leaves is now established. Continue working in est patt, while increasing on both edges of the complete leaves, and on the inner edges of the side leaves, as follows, in addition, work the number of chains between leaves as indicated:

ROWS 3–10: Work in est patt for 8 rows, working 2 dc in last st of first side leaf, in first and last st of each complete leaf, and in first st of second side leaf on every odd row; in addition, work 9 chs between leaves on Rows 3–4 and 8 chs between leaves on the following 6 rows.

From now on, each leaf is worked separately. When starting each leaf, be careful to always have the same side of the work facing you for each leaf.

SIDE LEAF 1

Start from the outer edge.

ROWS 1–7: Continue working in est patt over next 7 rows, working dc2tog over the last 2 sts on 1st, 5th, and 7th rows and working even on rows in between.

ROW 8: *Sizes 37½ (44½)" (95 [112.5] cm only:* Ch 3, dc in next st. Fasten off. *Sizes 34 (41)" (86.5 [104] cm) only:* Ch 3, dc in next st, finish row in est patt. Fasten off.

COMPLETE LEAF

Decrease at both edges of each complete leaf. From Row 5, the first decrease is worked as follows: Ch 2, sk 1st st, dc in next st. On the following row, do not work into the ch-2 (decreased stitch). (This decrease mirrors the dc2tog at the other edge).

ROW 1: Attach yarn with a dc2tog over first 2 sts, work in est patt until 2 sts remain, dc2tog over last 2 sts, turn.

ROWS 2–4: Work even.

ROW 5: Ch 2, sk 1st st, dc in next st, work in est patt until 2 sts remain, dc2tog over last 2 sts, turn.

ROW 6: Work even.

ROWS 7–8: Rep Rows 5–6.

ROW 9: Ch 2, sk 1st st, dc in next st, work lace panel, dc2tog over last 2 sts, turn.

ROW 10: Ch 3, dc in ch-1 sp, dc in next st, shell in next ch-1 sp, dc in next st, dc in ch-1 sp, dc in last st.

ROW 11: Ch 2, sk 1st st, dc in each of next 2 sts, shell in next ch-1 sp, dc in next st, dc2tog over last 2 sts.

ROW 12: Ch 2, sk 1st st, dc in next st, shell in next ch-1 sp, dc2tog over last 2 sts.

ROW 13: Ch 3, shell in next ch-1 sp, dc in last st. Fasten off.

SIDE LEAF 2

Start from the inner edge.

ROWS 1–7: Attach yarn with dc2tog over first 2 sts at leaf edge, continue working in est patt over next 7 rows, decreasing with (ch 2, sk 1 st, dc in next st) in the beginning of 5th and 7th rows. Do not work into ch-2 sp on return row.

ROW 8: *Sizes 34 (41)" (86.5 [104] cm) only:* Work in est patt until 2 sts rem, dc2tog over last 2 sts. Fasten off. *Sizes 37½ (44½)" (95 [112.5] cm) only:* Ch 3, 1 dc. Fasten off.

FRONT

Work same as Back to armhole shaping. Shape armholes same as Back, including transition of lace panels into plain stitches at top of armhole. *At the same time,* on Row 1 (1, 4, 4) of armhole shaping, transition the 1 (2, 2, 1) center lace panels to plain stitches. Starting on row 3 (3, 6, 6) of armhole shaping, shape front neck.

ROW 1: Work as for back armhole shaping, except over center 11 (11, 13, 13) sts, work hdc in first st, sc in next st, sl st in each of next 7 (7, 9, 9) sts, sc in next st, hdc in next st.

ROW 2: If neck edge is at beginning of row, sl st in each of first 3 (3, 3, 2) sts, ch 3, dc2tog over next 2 sts, continue as Row 4 (4, 7, 7) of back armhole shaping. If neck edge is at end of row, work as for Row 4 (4, 7, 7) on back armhole shaping until 5 (5, 5, 4) sts remain, dc2tog over next 2 sts, turn.

From here, each side of the front neck is worked separately. Continue as for back armhole shaping; *at the same time,* shape neck edge as follows. For decreases, if neck edge falls to beginning of row: ch 3, dc2tog over first 2 sts, continue in est patt. If neck edge falls to end of row: work until 2 sts remain, dc2tog over last 2 sts, turn.

ROW 3: Work even. Decrease 2 (2, 2, 2) sts at neck edge.

ROW 4: Work even. Decrease 0 (2, 0, 0) sts at neck edge.

ROW 5: Work even. Decrease 2 (0, 2, 2) sts at neck edge.

ROW 6: Work even. Decrease 0 (2, 0, 0) sts at neck edge.

ROW 7: Work even. Do not decrease at neck edge.

ROW 8: Work even. Decrease 2 (0, 2, 2) sts at neck edge.

ROWS 9–10: Work even. Do not decrease at neck edge.

ROW 11: Work even. Decrease 0 (2, 0 0) sts at neck edge.

ROW 12: Work even. Decrease 2 (0, 0, 0) sts at neck edge.

ROW 13: Work even. Decrease 0 (0, 2, 2) sts at neck edge.

ROWS 14–17: Work even. Do not decrease at neck edge.

ROW 18: Work even. Decrease 2 (0, 0, 0) sts at neck edge. *Shaping of front neck finished for size 34" (86.5 cm).*

ROW 19: Work even. Decrease (2, 0, 0) sts at neck edge. *Shaping of front neck finished for size 37½" (95 cm).*

ROW 20: Work even. Decrease (2, 2) sts at neck edge. *Shaping of front neck finished for sizes 41 (44½)" (104 [112.5] cm).*

Shape shoulders as for back. Working in same direction as Row 2, attach yarn and work second side of front neck.

Make the Front Leaves the same as the Back Leaves.

SLEEVES

Ch 60 (60, 75, 75).

ROW 1: Ch 3 (tch, does not count as a stitch here and throughout), working through both lps dc in each of next 3 ch, *work lace panel over next 9 ch, dc in each of next 6 ch; repeat from * 3 (3, 4, 4) more times, ending dc in each of last 3 ch, turn.

ROW 2: Ch 3, work in est patt.

Repeat Row 2. *At the same time,* increase as follows:

SLEEVE INCREASES

Increase 1 st at center of each side panel as follows:

Sizes 34 (44½)" (86.5 [112.5] cm) only: When sleeve measures 2¾ and 5½" (7 and 14 cm)—4 sts increased

Size 37½" (95 cm) only: When sleeve measures 2½, 4¾, and 7" (6, 12, and 18 cm)—6 sts increased.

Size 41" (104 cm) only: When sleeve measures 4¾" (12 cm)—2 sts increased.

When sleeve measures 7 (8, 8¾, 8¾)" (18 [20.5, 22, 22] cm), transition the outer 2 lace panels into plain stitches.

Work even until sleeve measures 7¾ (8¾, 9½, 9½)" (20 [22.5, 24, 24] cm).

SLEEVE CAP

ROW 1: Sl st in first 3 (4, 5, 6) sts, sc in next st, hdc in next st, work in est patt until 5 (6, 7, 8) sts remain, hdc in next st, sc in next st, turn leaving rem sts unworked.

SIZES 34 (37½, 41)" (86.5 [95, 104] CM) ONLY

ROW 2: Sl st in first 4 sts, ch 3, dc2tog over next 2 sts, work in est patt until 6 sts remain, dc2tog over next 2 sts, turn leaving rem sts unworked.

SIZE 44½" (112.5 CM) ONLY

ROW 2: Sl st in first 3 sts, sc in next st, hdc in next st, work in est patt until 5 sts remain, hdc in next st, sc in next st, turn leaving rem sts unworked.

SIZES 34 (41)" (86.5 [104] CM) ONLY

ROW 3: Sl st in first st, ch 3, dc2tog over next 2 sts, work in est patt until 3 sts remain, dc2tog over next 2 sts, turn leaving rem sts unworked.

SIZE 37½" (95 CM) ONLY

ROW 3: Ch 3, dc2tog over first 2 sts, work in est patt until 2 sts remain, dc2tog over last 2 sts, turn.

SIZE 44½" (112.5 CM) ONLY

ROW 3: Sl st in first 2 sts, ch 3, dc2tog over next 2 sts, work in est patt until 4 sts remain, dc2tog over next 2 sts, turn leaving rem sts unworked.

ALL SIZES

ROWS 4–6: Ch 3, dc2tog over first 2 sts, work in est patt until 2 sts remain, dc2tog over last 2 sts, turn.

SIZES 34 (37½)" (86.5 [95] CM) ONLY

ROW 7: Work even.

ROW 8: Ch 3, dc2tog over first 2 sts, work in est patt until 2 sts remain, dc2tog over last 2 sts, turn.

SIZE 41" (104 CM) ONLY

ROW 7: Ch 3, dc2tog over first 2 sts, work in est patt, transitioning the 2 outer remaining lace panels to plain stitches, dc2tog over last 2 sts, turn.

ROW 8: Work even.

SIZE 44½" (112.5 CM) ONLY

ROW 7: Ch 3, dc2tog over first 2 sts, work in est patt until 2 sts remain, dc2tog over last 2 sts, turn.

ROW 8: Work even, transitioning the 2 outer remaining lace panels to plain stitches.

ALL SIZES

ROWS 9–10: Ch 3, dc2tog over first 2 sts, work in est patt until 2 sts remain, dc2tog over last 2 sts, turn.

SIZE 34" (86.5 CM) ONLY

ROW 11: Work even. Transition center 2 lace panels into plain stitches.

SIZES 37½ (41)" (95 [104] CM) ONLY

ROW 11: Ch 3, dc2tog over first 2 sts, work in est patt until 2 sts remain, dc2tog over last 2 sts, turn.

SIZE 44½" (112.5 CM) ONLY

ROW 11: Work even.

SIZES 34 (41, 44½)" (86.5 [104, 112.5] CM) ONLY

ROW 12: Ch 3, dc2tog over first 2 sts, work in est patt until 2 sts remain, dc2tog over last 2 sts, turn.

SIZE 37½" (95 CM) ONLY

ROW 12: Work even. Transition center 2 lace panels into plain stitches.

ALL SIZES

ROW 13: Ch 3, dc2tog over first 2 sts, work in est patt until 2 sts remain, dc2tog over last 2 sts, turn.

SIZE 34" (86.5 CM) ONLY

ROW 14: Ch 1, sc in first st, hdc in next st, work in est patt until 2 sts remain. Hdc in next st, sc in last st, turn.

SIZES 37½ (41, 44½)" (95 [104, 112.5] CM) ONLY

ROW 14: Ch 3, dc2tog over first 2 sts, work in est patt until 2 sts remain, dc2tog over last 2 sts, turn.

SIZES 34 (37½)" (86.5 [95] CM) ONLY

ROW 15: Sl st in first 3 (1) sts, sc in next st, hdc in next st, dc in each of next 8 (14) sts, hdc in next st, sc in next st. *Size 34" (86.5 cm) only:* Fasten off. *Size 37½" (95 cm) only:* Turn.

SIZE 37½" (95 CM) ONLY

ROW 16: Sl st in first 2 sts, sc in next st, hdc in each of next 2 sts, dc in each of next 8 sts, hdc in each of next 2 sts, sc in next st. Fasten off.

SIZE 41" (104 CM) ONLY

ROW 15: Ch 3, dc2tog over first 2 sts, work in est patt, transitioning the center lace panel to plain stitches, dc2tog over last 2 sts, turn.

ROW 16: Sl st in first st, ch 1, hdc in next st, dc in each of next 19 sts, hdc in next st, turn.

ROW 17: Sl st in first 2 sts, sc in next st, hdc in next st, dc in each of next 13 sts, hdc in next st, sc in next st. Fasten off.

SIZE 44½" (112.5 CM) ONLY

ROW 15: Work even.

ROW 16: Ch 3, dc2tog over first 2 sts, work in est patt until 2 sts remain, dc2tog over last 2 sts, turn.

ROW 17: Ch 3, dc2tog over first 2 sts, work in est patt, transitioning the center lace panel into plain stitches, dc2tog over last 2 sts, turn.

ROW 18: Ch 1, sc in first st, hdc in next st, dc in each of next 17 sts, hdc in next st, sc in last st, turn.

ROW 19: Sl st in each of first 3 sts, sc in each of next 2 sts, hdc in each of next 11 sts, sc in each of next 2 sts. Fasten off.

SLEEVE LEAVES

Each sleeve leaf is worked separately and they are all identical. Turn the work and work Row 1 into the remaining loop of the base chain. For treatment of turning chains and decreases, see Back Leaves.

ROW 1: Attach the yarn with a dc in the second ch to the right of the first lace panel, dc in next st, work lace panel over next 9 sts (symmetrical to lace panel already worked on back), dc in each of next 2 sts, turn.

ROW 2: Ch 3, dc in first st, dc in next st, work lace panel, dc in next st, 2 dc in last st—2 sts increased.

ROW 3: Ch 3, dc in first st, dc in next 2 sts, work lace panel, dc in next 2 sts, 2 dc in last st—2 sts increased.

ROW 4: Work even.

ROW 5: Ch 2, sk 1st st, dc in next 3 sts, work lace panel, dc in next 2 sts, dc2tog over last 2 sts—2 sts decreased.

ROW 6: Ch 2, sk 1st st, dc in next 2 sts, work lace panel, dc in next st, dc2tog over last 2 sts—2 sts decreased.

ROW 7: Ch 2, sk 1st st, dc in next st, work lace panel, dc2tog over last 2 sts—2 sts decreased.

ROW 8: Ch 3, dc in ch-1 sp, dc in next st, shell in next ch-1 sp, dc in next st, dc in ch-1 sp, dc in last st.

ROW 9: Ch 2, sk 1st st, dc in next 2 sts, shell in next ch-1 sp, dc in next st, dc2tog over last 2 sts—2 sts decreased.

ROW 10: Ch 2, sk 1st st, dc in next st, shell in next ch-1 sp, dc2tog over last 2 sts—2 sts decreased.

ROW 11: Ch 3, shell in next ch-1 sp, dc in last st.

Fasten off.

FINISHING

Weave in yarn ends. Spray block garment pieces lightly to the dimensions shown in the schematic. (See Block It sidebar on page 66.)

BEADS

With sewing needle and matching sewing thread, sew seed beads to the outer border of the leaves, placing 2 beads on every row of dc (1 bead at the base of the stitch, 1 bead in the middle of the stitch). In the tip shell of each leaf, sew 1 bead to each stitch. Sew beads only on the inner, curved side of the side leaves of the body.

With yarn and yarn needle, sew the shoulder seams, the side seams and the sleeve seams. Sew sleeves to armholes.

Work 1 row of sc around the neck. When working into rows, work 2 sts into every row, and when working into stitches work 1 st into every stitch.

With sewing needle and matching sewing thread, sew seed beads around the neckline, placing 1 bead in every stitch.

CONNECTING SIDE LEAVES

In the top of Row 1 of the outer straight edge of the side leaf, attach the yarn with a slip stitch. *Ch 10. Attach with a slip stitch in the corresponding spot of the facing side leaf, on the other side of the side seam. Work 2 sl sts vertically into the outer stitch of the row above, placing 2nd sl st at top of row; repeat from * 15 times, leaving the last 2 rows unconnected.

PHOTO BY PER-OLOF PERSSON

designer in profile

annette petavy

One of the very first people to e-mail me when I started CrochetMe.com was Annette, a Swedish translator living in France. She wrote to me in English, apologizing for what struck me as perfect grammar and flowing prose. I assured her that her writing was excellent, and she started contributing articles right away. She once invited me to lunch in a fancy French cafe, and I've been saving up my pennies to take her up on that someday.

Perhaps inspired by the bland, gray, Stockholm suburb where she grew up, Annette has a keen eye for color and texture. She is a constant champion of creative exploration, especially in the simplest ways. It was in those drab suburbs that, as a kid, Annette would eat soil and seeds chased with water in the hope of growing a plant in her stomach. I went the other route and simply refused to eat fruit when I was a kid, out of fear of such a thing happening. To each her own, I suppose.

We do have a few things in common, though. To relax after a day working on crochet, Annette sews or knits. And here's what she thinks about crochet in the context of feminism:

"Any activity done mostly by women has been looked down upon for centuries. Saying that crocheting is an activity for old ladies who make doilies is not only reducing the craft to a small part of its possible applications, it's also showing disdain for the 'old ladies'—the mothers who brought us up, who stood behind us, who made everything we have possible. Here in France, many women who claim themselves 'feminists' still look down on traditional textile crafts. I am very proud to continue and develop an art that has been taught to me by my mother, with the help of my grandmother. When women had no possibility to express themselves as fine artists in the 'outside world,' they used their creativity to develop textile crafts at home. It's a heritage to be proud of. Since today it's possible, I have every intention to develop this heritage on a broader scene."

As of this writing, Annette has taken a break from translating to pursue crochet full-time.

KEEP TRACK OF ANNETTE'S WORK IN YOUR CHOICE OF THREE LANGUAGES AT ANNETTEPETAVY.COM.

ESSAY: generations

I did not grow up in a crafty household. In fact, my crafty plans always proved grander than my ability to produce them, like the larger-than-life-size cardboard robot I started to make in second grade but never finished because it was too big and unwieldy. When I was in grad school, hating where I lived and having only four friends, I was desperate for a hobby and I decided to make mosaics. This was not long after I started dating the man I eventually married. He's a crafty guy. His robot would not only have stood up on its own, it likely would have had opposable thumbs and rudimentary language. He took to mosaics like a duck to water, while I stared at my oddly misshapen coaster.

Several months after we moved to Vancouver I not-quite-literally pounced on my new friend Samantha, who mentioned taking a knitting class. Finally, a hobby that stuck. My husband had no interest in it, so I was safe from having it commandeered by more capable hands. A year later I started crocheting and a few weeks after that my mom and my grandmother came to visit.

My mom was keen to have me teach her to knit, a reversal of the usual passing of a craft from one generation to the next. I made her cast on, rip out, and cast on again for 45 minutes. She threatened my life, but I insisted that she know how to do it so she could start projects when she was back home, 3,000 miles away. When she began to actually knit, it became apparent that she'd learned at some earlier point, since she progressed quickly and efficiently knitting Continental-style, whereas I knit English. Easiest. Lesson. Ever.

All the while, my grandmother chatted and watched, and insisted she had no desire to crochet again (she'd never been a knitter and had stopped crocheting decades earlier).

Being pushy but not too pushy, I left yarn and a hook on the coffee table when my mom and I napped a lazy afternoon away. When we returned to the living room, my grandmother sat with a proud look on her face and held up the inches of double crochet she'd made. After the visit, I sent her an afghan's worth of yarn and a hook and she proceeded happily to make herself a small blanket, curtain ties, and various other useful household items.

Eight seems to be the magic crafty number. Ask a group of crocheters or knitters how old they were when they learned, and chances are the ones who learned as children started when they were eight. I'm one of the ones who learned when I was twenty-five. The magic has hardly been lost on me, however. I love that I can talk to my mom about our crafts; that we have this tangible thing to share as adults. I can learn from her steely resolve to complete projects that are slightly beyond her comfort level, and she can accept, usually without comment, that I always have a dozen projects in progress and rarely finish any.

It's special to share skills between generations, in whatever direction the knowledge is passed.

PHOTO BY NEIL PIPER

Grandma Shirley, Kim, and mom Shari, circa 1977.

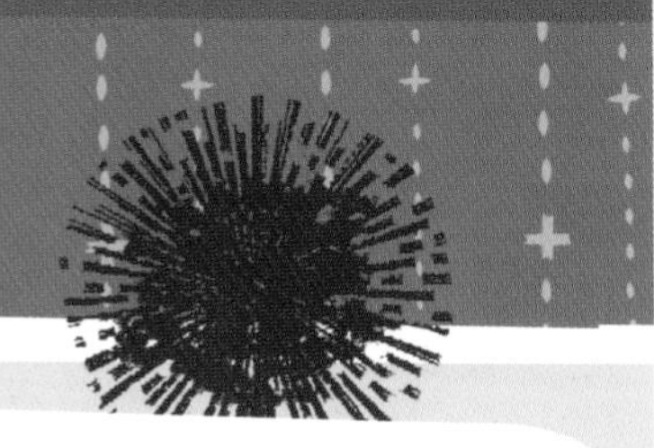

thigh *highs*

Cecily Keim

concentration rating 1 2 **3** 4

CECILY'S INSPIRATION

Tights, thigh highs, leggings! I can't remember when I didn't love these types of things. At the peak of my mania I loved to layer tights with socks, or ripped or lacy tights over solid tights—anything to stretch that miniskirt or pair of cutoffs into winter wear. Those were the days of clunky boots and teal-and-purple-streaked hair for me. I've changed a bit. I no longer rip tights on purpose for the effect, and I sent the not-so-flattering Warhol print tights to Goodwill. Now I'll settle for some nice, simple, textured stockings like these. I'll be wearing mine in gray, over a pair of solid-colored tights with a pair of open-toe shoes.

FINISHED SIZE

Custom fit. The foot is worked with a smaller hook to make a comfy sock. The hook size changes throughout the pattern to follow the shape of the leg and create loose single crochet stitches for the fishnet texture.

YARN

Cascade Fixation (98.3% cotton, 1.7% elastic; 100 yd [91 m]/50 g unstretched): # 8990 black, 5 skeins.

SUBSTITUTION: About 400–500 yd (366–457 m) of sock-weight (Super Fine #1) cotton with elastic.

HOOK

Size G/6 (4.0 mm) plus 4 additional hooks consecutively increasing in size, G/7 (4.5 mm), H/8 (5.0 mm), I/9 (5.5 mm), J/10 (6.0 mm). Change hook size if necessary to obtain the correct gauge.

NOTIONS

Stitch markers; yarn needle; ribbon (optional).

GAUGE

16 sc and 9 rows = 4" (10 cm) single crochet with smallest hook, unstretched.

+ PATTERN NOTES +

- Making a stocking with perfect fit takes some trial and error. Try the stocking on regularly as you work and follow the suggestions throughout the pattern as well as your own instinct for perfecting your fit. Keep notes where indicated of the number of rounds you work, increases, etc., so you can work the second stocking identical to the first.
- Use as many stitch markers as you need. When you mark a stitch, write it in your notes so you remember why you marked it.
- Unless otherwise instructed, the pattern is worked in a spiral without joining or turning at the end of each round.

STOCKING

START WITH THE TOES

Using smallest hook, make a foundation chain as long as the distance from your middle toe to your big toe. *Write down:* _______ number of chains in your foundation chain.

FOUNDATION ROW: Working into the ridge on the backside of the chain, sl st in each ridge loop across the chain. You now have a foundation row with two sets of loops, one on the top (the slip stitches) and one on the bottom (the foundation chain).

RND 1: Ch 1, rotate your work 180° and continue working through both top loops of the foundation chain, sc in ch across. Place a marker in the last sc. Rotate 180° again, sc into each sl st across. Place a marker in the last sc.

START WORKING INCREASES

Each increase round will add 4 stitches to the stitch count.

INCREASE RND: 2 sc in the next st, sc in each st until you reach the st before a marker. 2 sc in the st before the marked st, 1 sc in the marked st (move marker up), 2 sc in the next st, sc in each st across until you reach the st before the next marker, 2 sc in the st before the marked st, 1 sc in the marked st (move marker up). Markers should be in the stitch between increases on each end of the round. Rep the Increase Round until the stocking foot stretches nicely over your toes and reaches the bottom of your toes when stretched a bit. *Write down:* _______ number of increase rounds worked. _______ stitch count for last round.

EVEN RND: Sc in each st around. If the stocking foot is too narrow, work 1 more Increase Round. *Write down:* If you used an extra increase round. _______ Stitch count for the round. Rep Even Round until the stocking foot fits to just past the middle of the arch of your foot when stretched a bit. *Tip:* Use a marker at the beginning of each round to help keep track of the rounds. *Write down:* _______ how many even rounds used. _______ how many rounds total on the foot so far.

HEEL

Fold the stocking foot flat so that it looks like the bottom of your foot, with the middle of the foundation row centered at the toe. The open side of the folded stocking foot, with the end of your last round, is the bottom of the foot. Place a marker in the stitch on the right and left corner of the bottom of the foot. To build a heel, you will start to work from here in rows between the markers. It doesn't matter where the last round ended, simply work to the next marker:

ROW 1: Sc in each st to the next marker of the stocking foot, turn.

ROW 2: Ch 1, sc in each st to opposite marker, turn.

ROW 3: Ch 1, sc in each sc until the last st, omit the last st, turn.

Repeat Row 3 until the number of stitches in the row is equal to the number of stitches in the foundation chain (refer to your notes).

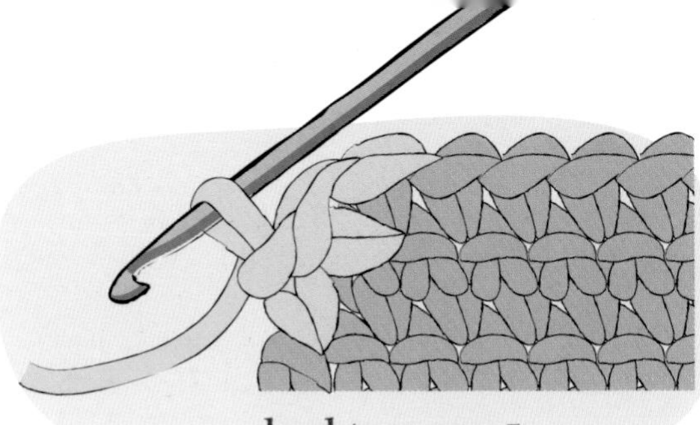
heel turn row 1

TURN THE HEEL

TURN ROW 1: Ch 1, sc in each st from the previous row, work 1 sc in the side of the previous row and 1 sc in the unworked sc of the row previous to that, turn (see illustration above).

Repeat Turn Row 1 until you meet back up with the last round before heel shaping began.

FINISH HEEL TURN: Switch to next hook size .5 mm bigger, ch 1, sc in each st around stocking. *Write down:* _______ Stitch count for the round.

Try it on. Is the body of the foot too baggy or too tight? Is the foot too long before the heel starts or too short? Here are some suggestions for reworking the foot if the fit isn't quite right yet:

- *Too baggy:* If the foot is too baggy, pinch the fabric while on your foot. How many stitches did you pinch? That is how many increase stitches you need to reduce from your toe increase rounds. For example, if you pinched 4 stitches, start working even rounds 1 round earlier.
- *Too tight:* You need to add increases. Go back to the toe increase rounds and work the number of increase rounds (likely only 1 or 2) needed to add the required width to your stocking foot. Be sure to adjust the number of even rounds before the heel turn to accommodate for the change in the number of increase rounds.
- *Too long:* If the foot is too long, you need to decrease the number of even rounds before the heel turn. Pinch the fabric while on your foot. If you're able to pinch 2 rounds, work 2 fewer even rounds before the heel turn.
- *Too short:* If the foot of your stocking is too short, you need to add more Even Rounds before the heel turn.

Write down: Any problems you have with your stocking foot and what actions to take to fix them. If you rework the foot, note all changes and new round or stitch counts that result. Once you have the fit right, move on to working the shaping for the leg.

ANKLE DECREASES

RND 1: There will be a crook on each side of the foot where the ankle would be. Mark the stitch at each crook. Sc in each unmarked st, sc2tog over 2 sts at each marked st.

RND 2: Place markers 1" (2.5 cm) to either side of each ankle decrease (4 markers total). Sc in each unmarked st around, work 2 sc at each marked st.

RND 3: Sc in each st around.

RND 4: Switch to next hook size .5 mm bigger, sc in each st around.

LEG DECREASES

Decreasing at the back of the leg of the stocking helps create a shape that follows the contour of your leg.

RND 1: Count out 12 sts centered at the back of the leg; place a marker at each side of the 12 sts. Sc in each st until the first marked stitch near back of the leg, [sc2tog over the next 2 sts] 6 times, sc in each st to the end of the round.

RND 2: Count out 4 sts centered at the back of the leg; place a marker at each side of the 4 sts. Sc in each st until the first marked stitch near back of the leg, [sc2tog over the next 2 sts] 2 times, sc in each st to the end of the round.

RNDS 3–4: Sc in each st around.

Try it on. How does the leg shaping fit? If the fabric looks strained, rip back and reduce the number of decreases in Round 1 of the Leg

Decreases. *Write down:* Any changes you make to the number of decreases used to shape the leg.

Continue working stocking leg: change to next hook size .5 mm bigger and work even rounds until the fabric of the stocking starts to strain from the curve of the calf.

CALF INCREASES

* Sc in each of next 4 sts, work 2 sc in next st. Rep from * around.

STOCKING LEG

LEG RND: Change to next hook size .5 mm bigger, sc in each st around. Repeat the Leg Rnd until the stocking fits to a bit above the knee. *Write down:* _______ how many rounds worked.

Try it on. If the fabric is too tight around the calf, make a guess as to how many increases you need and try spacing them out evenly for a second round of calf increases before switching to the largest hook. Remember you want enough stretch and play in the fabric to create a fishnet texture, so don't add too many increases! *Write down:* _______ any increases added to adjust for your fit.

Fasten off. Complete the second stocking same as the first.

FINISHING

Weave in yarn ends. The stockings will stretch and take on the shape of your legs. If you want to reshape them, handwash and roll gently in a towel to absorb excess water. Place in a pillow case and tumble dry on the lowest heat until they've returned to their original shape.

You can weave ribbon through the top of the stocking for a tie to help hold them up.

designer in profile

cecily keim

Cecily and I met for the first time at a Crochet Guild of America conference in the fall of 2004. Two months later we decided to write a book together (*Teach Yourself Visually Crocheting*). It was sort of magic like that.

With a background in acting, Cecily does the best impressions of anyone I've ever known. She also calls people "sweetie," and it's, well, really sweet. She lives in Los Angeles, in an apartment she goes out of her way to keep comfortable and creative with pretty colors, comfy furniture, cats, and an adorable boyfriend.

Cecily is all about encouraging creativity and exploration, and she loves to connect with people about it, especially through crochet. She says it best herself: "No matter where I go, if I pull out my crochet I'm likely to find myself chatting with someone about the work in my hands. This is what I have in common with everyone: I make things. Just like the stranger sitting next to me on the airplane. I get to hear about grandmothers and aunties and all sorts of things that matter to a person and it all starts because I've got a hook in hand and people connect with that. It's a way of connecting with family, and it's a way of connecting with someone who doesn't speak the same language. Whether you make things by hand out of necessity or as a hobby, it's a common link. Call me cheesy, but I've found this link, this human impulse to create with our own hands, far more important and less fleeting in the large scheme of things than politics and other differences. This is why I'm grateful to work in crochet and make things. It keeps my priorities on something I feel matters."

CECILY BLOGS AT SUCHSWEETHANDS.COM, WHERE SHE EXPLORES CREATIVITY IN GENERAL, AND CROCHET SPECIFICALLY.

comfy *cardi*

Robyn Chachula

concentration rating 1 2 **3** 4

ROBYN'S INSPIRATION

This cardi was inspired by my two daily needs: to crochet fun lacy patterns and to keep warm because I am always cold. I originally dreamed up this design at work, watching all the women in my office walk around in ugly cardigans, coats, or large shirts because they were cold. I asked myself, "Why should they have to look silly in their 'office sweaters'"? Why not make a pretty office sweater you could wear with everything every day? Thus, the comfi cardi was born.

FINISHED SIZE

BUST CIRCUMFERENCE: 32 (35, 38, 41) (81.5 [89, 96.5, 104] cm). Sweater is designed to be close-fitting.

YARN

Blue Sky Alpacas Alpaca and Silk (50% alpaca, 50% silk; 146 yd [133 m] 50 g): #29 Amethyst, 9 (10, 12, 13) skeins

SUBSTITUTION: About 1,312, (1,422, 1750, 1859) yd (1,200 [1,300, 1,600, 1,700] m) sportweight (Fine #2) alpaca/silk blend.

HOOK

Size G/6 (4.25 mm). Change hook size if necessary to obtain the correct gauge.

NOTIONS

Yarn needle; 1¼" (3.2 cm) diameter button.

GAUGE

30 sts and 12 rows = 4¾" (12 cm) in Lacy Diamond Stitch pattern (see Special Stitches on page 92).

+ SPECIAL STITCHES +

V-STITCH (V-ST): (Dc, ch 3, dc) all into same stitch.

DOUBLE CROCHET CLUSTER (DC-CL): Yo, insert hook in first dc of next dc group, yo and pull up lp, yo and pull through 2 lps on hook, yo, insert hook in last dc of same group, yo and pull up lp, yo and pull through 2 lps on hook, yo and pull through 3 lps on hook.

LACY DIAMOND STITCH PATTERN

Ch 33.

ROW 1: Sk 3 ch from hook (counts as dc), dc in each of next 2 ch, *sk 2 ch, V-st in next ch (see above), sk 2 ch, dc in each of next 5 ch; rep from * across, ending with dc in each of last 3 ch, turn.

ROW 2: Ch 2 (counts as first leg of dc-cl), sk first 2 sts, dc in next st, ch 2, 5 dc in ch-3 sp of next V-st, ch 2, *dc-cl over next 5-dc group (see above), ch 2, 5 dc in ch-3 sp of next V-st, ch 2; rep from * across to last 3 dc, dc-cl over last 3 dc, turn.

ROW 3: Ch 4 (counts as dc, ch 1), dc in same dc-cl, sk ch-2 sp, dc in each of next 5 dc, sk ch-2 sp, *V-st in next dc-cl, sk ch-2 sp, dc in each of next 5 dc, sk ch-2 sp; rep from * to last dc-cl, (dc, ch 1, dc) in next dc-cl, turn.

ROW 4: Ch 3 (counts as dc), 2 dc in ch-1 sp, ch 2, dc-cl over next 5-dc group, ch 2, *5 dc in ch-3 sp of next V-st, ch 2, dc-cl over 5-dc group, ch 2; rep from * across, ending with 3 dc in tch sp, turn.

ROW 5: Ch 3 (counts as dc), dc in each of next 2 dc, sk ch-2 sp, V-st in next dc-cl, sk ch-2 sp, *dc in each of next 5 dc, sk ch-2 sp, V-st in next dc-cl, sk ch-2 sp; rep from * across ending with dc in each of last 3 dc, turn.

Repeat Rows 2–5 to desired length.

SC-BLO: Work sc through back lp only.

DC-BLO: Work dc through back lp only.

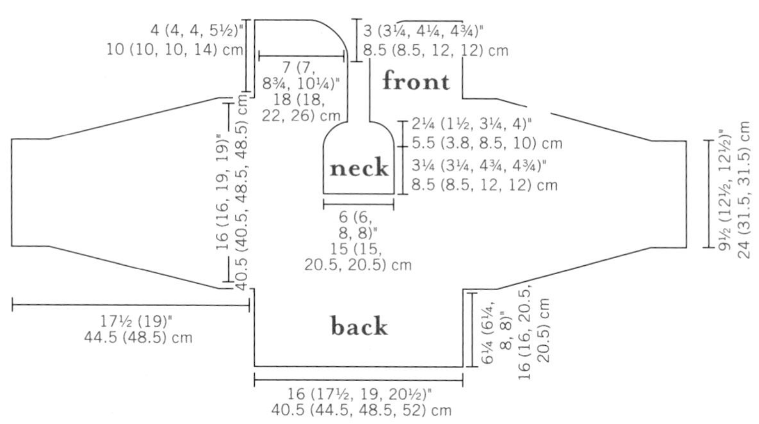

lacy diamond stitch pattern

Row Repeat

one stitch pattern repeat

Key

- chain
- double crochet
- double crochet decrease

+ PATTERN NOTES +

- The body and arms are constructed in one piece for seamless shoulders. The ribbing is added during finishing.

SWEATER

BACK

Ch 103 (113, 123, 133).

ROW 1 (RS): Follow Row 1 of lacy diamond stitch patt (see Special Stitches)—10 (11, 12, 13) V-sts total.

ROWS 2–17 (17, 21, 21): Repeat Rows 2–5 of lacy diamond stitch patt 4 (4, 5, 5) times.

ARMS

To add stitches for the arm, you will remove the hook at the beginning of each row, add chain stitches to the opposite end, fasten off and pick up the dropped loop to continue.

ROW 1: Drop yarn, join new yarn to opposite end with sl st, ch 18 (18, 28, 28), fasten off. Pick up row again, ch 22 (22, 32, 32), sk first 5 chs (counts as dc, ch 2), dc in each of next 5 ch, ch 2, dc-cl (see Special Stitches) over next 5 chs, ch 2, dc in each of next 5 ch, ch 2, dc-cl over next ch and last dc of next 3-dc group, ch 2, 5 dc in ch-3 sp of next V-st (see Special Stitches), ch 2, *dc-cl over next 5-dc group, ch 2, 5 dc in ch-3 sp of V-st, ch 2; rep from * to last 3 dc, dc-cl over first dc of 3-dc group and second ch, ch 2, dc in each of next 5 chs, ch 2, dc-cl over next 5 chs, ch 2, dc in each of next 5 chs, ch 2, dc in last ch, turn—13 (14, 17, 18) dc-cl total.

ROW 2: Drop yarn, join new yarn to opposite end with sl st, ch 10, fasten off. Pick up row again, ch 16, dc in 7th ch from hook (counts as V-st), sk 2 ch, dc in each of next 5 ch, sk last 2 ch, V-st in first dc, continue in est patt for Row 3 of lacy diamond stitch patt to last dc (tch), V-st in last dc, sk 2 ch, dc in each of next 5 ch, sk 2 ch, V-st in last ch, turn—17, (18, 21, 22) V-sts total.

ROW 3: Drop yarn, join new yarn to opposite end with sl st, ch 8, fasten off. Pick up row again, ch 11, sk first 3 chs (counts as dc), 2 dc in next ch, dc in each of next 2 chs, ch 2, dc-cl over next 5 chs, ch 2, 5 dc in next V-st, continue in est patt for Row 4 of lacy diamond stitch patt to last V-st, 5 dc in V-st, ch 2, dc-cl over next 5 chs, ch 2, dc in each of next 2 chs, 3 dc in last ch, turn—18 (19, 22, 23) dc-cl total.

ROW 4: Drop yarn, join new yarn to opposite end with sl st, ch 8, fasten off. Pick up row again, ch 10, sk first 3 chs (counts as dc), dc in each of next 2 chs, sk 2 ch, V-st in next ch, sk last 2 ch, dc in each of next 5 dc, continue in est patt for Row 5 of lacy diamond stitch patt to last dc, dc in last dc, sk 2 ch, V-st in next ch, sk 2 ch, dc in each of last 3 ch, turn—19 (20, 23, 24) V-sts total.

ROW 5: Drop yarn, join new yarn to opposite end with sl st, ch 8, fasten off. Pick up row again, ch 12, sk first 5 sts (counts as dc, ch 2), dc in each of next 5 ch, ch 2, dc-cl over next ch and last dc of 3-dc group, work in est patt for Row 2 of lacy diamond stitch patt to last 3 dc, dc-cl over last 3 dc and first 2 ch, ch 2, dc in each of next 5 chs, ch 2, dc in last ch, turn—19 (20, 23, 24) dc-cl total.

ROWS 6–8: Repeat Rows 2–4 of Arms.

ROW 9: Drop yarn, join new yarn to opposite end with sl st, ch 18, fasten off. Pick up row again, ch 22, sk first 5 chs, (counts as dc, ch 2), dc in each of next 5 chs, ch 2, dc-cl over next 5 chs, ch 2, dc in each of next 5 ch, ch 2, dc-cl over next ch and last dc of next 3-dc group, ch 2, 5 dc in ch-3 sp of V-st, ch 2, *dc-cl over next 5-dc group, ch 2, 5 dc in ch-3 sp of V-st, ch 2; rep from * across to last 3 dc, dc-cl over last 3 dc and first 2 ch, ch 2, dc in each of next 5 dc, ch 2, dc-cl over next 5 chs, ch 2, dc in each of next 5 chs, ch 2, dc in last ch, turn—31 (32, 35, 36) dc-cl tøtal.

ROWS 10–19 (19, 23, 23): Beg with patt Row 3, work lacy diamond stitch patt 2 (2, 3, 3) times, then work Rows 2–4 once.

RIGHT ARM AND NECK OPENING

ROW 1: Ch 3 (counts as dc), dc in each of next 2 dc, V-st in next dc-cl, *dc in each of next 5 dc, V-st in next dc-cl; rep from * across for 14 (14, 14, 15) V-sts total. *Sizes 32 (41)" (81.5 [104] cm) only:* dc in each of next 3 dc, turn; *sizes 35 (38)" (89 [96.5] cm) only:* dc in each of next 5 dc, (dc, ch 1, dc) in next dc-cl, turn. Leave remaining stitches unworked.

ROW 2: *Sizes 32 (41)" (81.5 [104] cm) only:* ch 2 (counts as first leg of dc-cl), sk next dc, dc in next dc; *sizes 35 (38)" (89 [96.5] cm) only:* ch 3 (counts as dc), 2 dc in ch-1 sp, ch 2, dc-cl over 5-dc group; *all sizes:* *ch 2, 5 dc in ch-3 sp of V-st, ch 2, dc-cl over next 5-dc group; rep from * across ending with dc-cl over last 3-dc group, turn.

ROW 3: Ch 4 (counts as dc, ch 1), dc in same dc-cl, dc in each of next 5 dc, *V-st in next dc-cl, dc in each of next 5 dc; rep from * to last dc-cl. *Sizes 32 (41)" (81.5 [104] cm) only:* (dc, ch 1, dc) in next dc-cl, turn; *sizes 35 (38)" (89 [96.5] cm) only:* V-st in next dc-cl, dc in each of last 3 dc, turn.

ROW 4: *Sizes 32 (41)" (81.5 [104] cm) only:* ch 3 (counts as dc), 2 dc in ch-1 sp, ch 2, dc-cl over next 5-dc group; *sizes 35 (38)" (89 [96.5] cm) only:* ch 2 (counts as first leg of dc cl), sk next dc, dc in next dc; *all sizes:* ch 2, *5 dc in ch-3 sp of V-st, ch 2, dc-cl over next 5-dc group, ch 2; rep from * across, ending 3 dc in tch sp, turn.

ROW 5: Ch 3 (counts as dc), dc in each of next 2 dc, *V-st in next dc-cl, dc in each of next 5 dc; rep from * to last dc-cl. *Sizes 32 (41)" (81.5 [104] cm) only:* V-st in next dc-cl, dc in each of last 3 dc, turn; *sizes 35 (38)" (89 [96.5] cm) only:* (dc, ch1, dc) in next dc-cl, turn.

ROWS 6–10: Repeat Rows 2–5 above 1 (1, 2, 2) more time(s), then repeat Row 2 once more.

ROW 11: Ch 4 (counts as dc, ch 1), dc in same dc-cl, dc in each of next 5 dc, *V-st in next dc-cl, dc in each of next 5 dc rep from * to last dc-cl. *Sizes 32 (41)" (81.5 [104] cm) only:* V-st in next dc-cl, turn. *Sizes 35 (38)" (89 [96.5] cm) only:* V-st in next dc-cl, dc in each of last 3 dc, turn—14 (14, 14, 15) V-st total.

ROW 12: *Sizes 32 (41)" (81.5 [104] cm) only:* Ch 5 (counts as dc, ch 2), 5 dc in ch-3 sp, ch 2, dc-cl over 5-dc group; *sizes 35 (38)" (89 [96.5] cm) only:* ch 2 (counts as first leg of dc cl), sk next dc, dc in next dc; *all sizes:* ch 2, *5 dc in ch-3 sp of V-st, ch 2, dc-cl over 5-dc group, ch 2; rep from * across, ending with 3 dc in tch sp, turn—14 (14, 14, 15) dc-cl total.

ROW 13: Ch 3 (counts as dc), dc in each of next 2 dc, *V-st in next dc-cl, dc in each of next 5 dc; rep from * to last dc-cl. *Sizes 32 (41)" (81.5 [104] cm) only:* V-st in 3rd ch of tch, turn—15 (15, 15, 16) V-st total; *sizes 35 (38)" (89 [96.5] cm) only:* V-st in next dc-cl, turn.

ARM SHAPING

ROW 14: Ch 5 (counts as dc, ch 2), 5 dc in ch-3 sp of V-st, ch 2, *dc-cl over next 5-dc group, ch 2, 5 dc in ch-3 sp of V-st, ch 2; rep from * to last 3 V-st, ch 2, dc-cl over next 5-dc group, leave remaining sts unworked. Fasten off, turn—13 (13 13, 14) dc-cl total.

ROW 15: Skip first dc-cl, join yarn to next dc-cl, ch 3 (counts as dc), dc in each of next 5 dc, *V-st in next dc-cl, dc in each of next 5 dc; rep from * across, V-st in 3rd ch of tch, turn—12 (12, 12, 13) V-st total.

ROW 16: Ch 5 (counts as dc, ch 2), *5 dc in ch-3 sp of V-st, ch 2, dc-cl over next 5-dc group, ch 2; rep from * to last V-st, 3 dc in last V-st. Fasten off. Turn—11 (11, 11, 12) dc-cl total.

ROW 17: Skip first dc-cl and next 2 dc, join yarn in next dc, ch 3, dc in each of next 2 dc, *V-st in next dc-cl, dc in each of next 5 dc; rep from * across. *Sizes 32 (35)" (81.5 [89] cm) only:* (dc, ch 1, dc) in 3rd ch of tch, turn; *sizes 38 (41)" (96.5 [104] cm) only:* V-st in 3rd ch of tch, turn—10 (10, 11, 12) V-st total.

ROW 18: *Sizes 32 (35)" (81.5 [89] cm) only:* ch 3 (counts as dc), 2 dc in ch-1 sp, ch 2;

sizes 38 (41)" (96.5 [104] cm) only: ch 5 (counts as dc, ch 2), 5 dc in ch-3 sp of V-st, ch 2; *all sizes:* *dc-cl over next 5-dc group, ch 2, 5 dc in ch-3 sp of V-st, ch 2; rep from * to last 2 V-st, ch 2, dc-cl over next 5 dc. Fasten off, leaving rem V-st unworked, turn—10 (10, 11, 12) dc-cl total.

ROW 19: Skip first dc-cl, join yarn in next dc-cl, ch 3 (counts as dc), dc in each of next 5 dc, *V-st in next dc-cl, dc in each of next 5 dc; rep from * to last dc-cl. *Sizes 32 (35)" (81.5 [89] cm) only:* dc in each of next 3 dc, turn; *sizes 38 (41)" (96.5 [104] cm) only:* dc in each of next 5 dc, V-st in 3rd ch of tch, turn—8 (8, 10, 11) V-st total.

ROW 20: *Sizes 32 (35)" (81.5 [89] cm) only:* ch 2 (counts as first leg of dc cl), sk dc, dc in next dc, ch 2; *sizes 38 (41)" (96.5 [104] cm) only:* ch 5 (counts as dc, ch 2); *all sizes:* *5 dc in ch-3 sp of V-st, ch 2, dc-cl over 5-dc group, ch 2; rep from * across to last V-st, 3 dc in last V-st. Fasten off, turn—7 (7, 9, 10) dc-cl total.

ROW 21: Skip first dc-cl and next 2 dc, join yarn in next dc, ch 3, dc in each of next 2 dc, *V-st in next dc-cl, dc in each of next 5 dc; rep from * across. *Sizes 32 (35)" (81.5 [89] cm) only:* (dc, ch 1, dc) in next dc-cl, turn; *sizes 38 (41)" (96.5 [104] cm) only:* (dc, ch 1, dc) in 3rd ch of tch, turn—6 (6, 8, 9) V-st total.

RIGHT FRONT PANEL

ROW 1: Ch 3 (counts as dc), 2 dc in ch-1 sp, ch 2, *dc-cl over next 5-dc group, ch 2, 5 dc in ch-3 sp of V-st, ch 2; rep from * to last 3, (3, 4, 4) V-st, ch 2, dc-cl over next 5 dc, turn. Leave remaining sts unworked (5, 5, 6, 7 dc-cl total).

ROW 2: Ch 4 (counts as dc, ch 1), dc in same dc-cl, dc in each of next 5 dc, *V-st in next dc-cl, dc in each of next 5 dc; rep from * across, ending with dc in each of last 3 dc, turn.

ROW 3: Ch 2 (counts as first leg of dc-cl), sk next dc, dc in next dc, ch 2, *5 dc in ch-3 sp of V-st, ch 2, dc-cl over next 5-dc group, ch 2; rep from * across, ending with 3 dc in tch sp, turn.

ROW 4: Ch 3 (counts as dc), dc in each of next 2 dc, *V-st in next dc-cl, dc in each of next 5 dc ; rep from * across, ending with (dc, ch 1, dc) in last dc, turn.

ROW 5: Ch 3 (counts as dc), 2 dc in ch-1 sp, ch 2, *dc-cl over next 5-dc group, ch 2, 5 dc in ch-3 sp of V-st, ch 2; rep from * to last V-st, dc-cl over last 3-dc group, turn.

ROWS 6–7: Repeat Rows 2–3 above.

ROW 8: Ch 3 (counts as dc), dc in each of next 2 dc, *V-st in next dc-cl, dc in each of next 5 dc; rep from * across, ending with dc in last dc, turn.

ROW 9: Ch 3 (counts as dc), sk next 4 dc, dc in next dc, ch 2, *5 dc in ch-3 sp of V-st, ch 2, dc-cl over next 5-dc group, ch 2; rep from * across, ending with dc-cl over last 3-dc group, turn—3 (3, 4, 5) dc-cl total.

ROW 10: Ch 4 (counts as dc, ch 1), dc in same dc-cl, *dc in each of next 5 dc, V-st in next dc-cl; rep from * across, ending with dc in last dc, turn.

ROW 11: Ch 3 (counts as dc), sk next 4 dc, dc in next dc, ch 2, *5 dc in ch-3 sp of V-st, ch 2, dc-cl over 5-dc group, ch 2; rep from * across, ending with 3 dc in tch sp, turn.

ROWS 12–15: Repeat Rows 8–11 once, (once, twice, twice). Fasten off—3 (3, 3, 4) dc-cl total.

LEFT FRONT PANEL

SIZE 32 (41)" (81.5 [104] CM) ONLY

ROW 1: Skip 4 (5) dc-cl on row 19 of arm from neck opening, skip next ch 2 and 2 dc, join yarn in next dc, ch 3 (counts as dc), continue in est patt for Row 5 of lacy diamond stitch patt, turn.

SIZE 35 (38)" (89 [96.5] CM) ONLY

ROW 1: Skip 3 (4) dc-cl on row 19 of arm from neck opening, join yarn in next dc, ch 4 (counts as dc, ch 1), dc in same dc-cl, ch 2, continue in est patt for Row 5 of lacy diamond stitch patt, turn.

Continue with arm and panel shaping by reversing Right Front Panel shaping.

FINISHING

Weave in yarn ends. With right sides together and using a yarn needle, whipstitch arm and side seams. Turn right side out.

CUFFS

Ribbing is connected to the sleeve by working sl sts into the row ends.

With WS facing, join yarn at arm opening side seam with sl st, ch 15.

ROW 1: Sc in 2nd ch from hook and in each ch across, sl st twice onto edge of arm opening (first sl st joins row to arm, second sl st counts as ch 1), turn.

ROW 2: Skip 2 sl st, sc-blo (see Special Stitches) in each sc across, turn.

ROW 3: Ch 1, sc-blo in each sc across, sl st three times on to edge of arm opening (first sl st joins row to arm, next 2 sl st counts as ch 2), turn.

ROW 4: Skip 3 sl st, dc-blo (see Special Stitches) in each sc across, turn.

ROW 5: Ch 1, sc-blo in each dc across, sl st twice on to edge of arm opening, turn.

Repeat Rows 2–5 evenly around arm opening for cuff.

Whipstitch last row and first row together. Weave in ends.

COLLAR AND BODY RIBBING

With wrong side facing, join yarn at middle of neck opening, ch 18, turn. Work ribbing as for Cuffs around body to buttonhole location (right front panel at end of increase shaping for neck).

BUTTONHOLE ROW 2: Skip 2 sl st, sc-blo in each sc across to last 7 sc, ch 3, skip next 3 sc, sc-blo in each of last 4 sc, turn.

BUTTONHOLE ROW 3: Ch 1, sc-blo in each of next 4 sc, 3 sc in ch-3 sp, sc-blo in each sc across, sl st 3 times on to edge of body, turn.

Continue in ribbing pattern evenly around body. Fasten off.

Whipstitch first and last rows together. Weave in ends. Sew button onto opposite side of ribbing using buttonhole placement as a guide.

Block ribbing if necessary (see Block It sidebar on page 66).

technically speaking: SHAPING

Although crochet has been around for a good long time, in many ways we're experiencing a new era of the craft. The vast majority of crocheted garments used to be unsophisticated. They were stiff, heavy, bulky, and boxy. To say they were unflattering would be an understatement. Because of this, crocheters have not paid a huge amount of attention to garment construction relative to, say, sewers and knitters.

You might have surmised already that my goal with this book is to spark something in your approach to your crochet—whether it's a realization about gauge, a thoughtfulness about hook size, or anything else you might not have considered before. Well, it's entirely possible you've never given a moment's thought to shaping a garment.

Let's start by thinking about the shape of you. You have curves. Where are they? How does a boxy, bulky sweater make them look? To illustrate, I'll answer these questions about myself.

I have curves. I have a small waist relative to my bust and hip measurements, and my hips are larger than my bust measurement might prefer. Boxy sweaters take on the dimensions of my widest parts (my butt and hips), which makes all of me look a size or two larger than I really am. Likewise, an empire waist accentuates my ample bust, hides my smaller waist, and widens to that pesky widest part. If I were to wear an empire waist to a family reunion, all my relatives would wonder when the baby is due. But, when I wear an A-line skirt with a boat-neck top that's shaped at the waist, people ask me if I've lost weight. Aha!

We owe it to our curves to work together. It might be as simple as taking a boxy sweater pattern and adding some waist shaping. This is not as difficult as you think. Examine some of the patterns in this book. And read Annette Petavy's two-part article about it on CrochetMe.com (February/March and April/May 2005). Eliminating the bulk at your waist will do wonders for making your crocheted garments flatter your body. Need extra fabric? Increase instead of decrease. Check out Megan Granholm's Five O'Clock Tank pattern on page 98. She included optional darts for C and D cups to accommodate the Tunisian crochet stitch, which doesn't have much give. I tried on the tank that's modeled. My breasts squooshed out the sides, and I became very appreciative of Megan's attention to detail.

If you're short, don't feel obligated to make a tunic a tunic. Feel free to shorten that baby into a hip-length sweater. If you're tall, make it longer. And remember, crochet can be sculptural. You're not limited to working increases and decreases at the side seams of your garment. You can work darts. You can use short-rows. Learn to make each project your own.

For more information about shaping, check out *Couture Crochet Workshop: Mastering Fit, Fashion, and Finesse* by Lily M. Chin (Interweave Press).

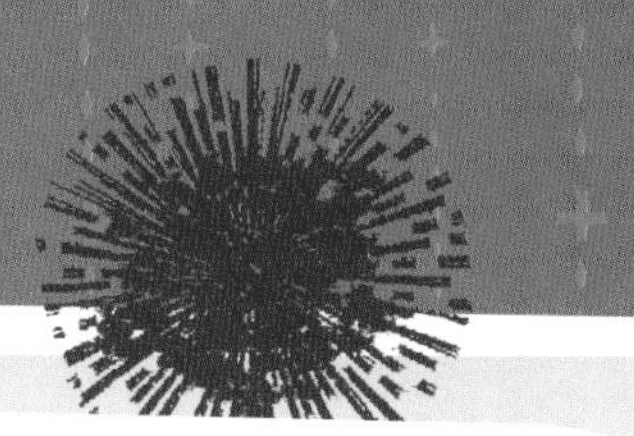

five o'clock *tank*

Megan Granholm

concentration rating 1 2 3 4

MEGAN'S INSPIRATION

I've always been pleased with the way bamboo yarn drapes when it's crocheted, not to mention that it's all natural. So it was a short hop from hugging the yarn every time I went to my local yarn shop to using it in a pattern. The design was born from one of those Friday nights when I was late coming home from work and would have loved to change out of my button-up work blouse into something a little sexier for my hot date with my husband. I'm not a tiny little body anymore either, so I wanted the option of showing off my neck and cleavage but not my spare tire. The lace is dense enough that I don't feel self-conscious about wearing it without a cami underneath.

FINISHED SIZE

BUST CIRCUMFERENCE: 28 (30, 34, 36, 38)" (71 [76, 86.5, 91.5, 96.5] cm), with optional darts for C and D cups. Sweater is designed to be close-fitting.

YARN

South West Trading Company Bamboo (100% bamboo; 250 yd (229 m)/100 g), #521 fuchsia, 3 (3, 4, 4, 5) skeins.

SUBSTITUTION: About 675 (755, 835, 915, 995) yd (617 [690, 764, 837, 910] m) of DK weight (Light #3) yarn.

HOOK

Size E (3.5mm) and size E (3.5mm) Tunisian (Afghan) hook. Change hook size if necessary to obtain the correct gauge.

NOTIONS

Yarn needle; stitch marker; one ¾" (2 cm) button; short invisible zipper (optional).

GAUGE

2 Shells = 5" (12.5 cm). *Tunisian crochet:* 24 Tsts and 28 rows = 4" (10 cm) with Tunisian hook (see Special Stitches, page 100).

+ SPECIAL STITCHES +

SHELL (SH): Work (dc, ch 2, dc, ch 2, dc) all in same st.

TUNISIAN CROCHET: This pattern uses the Tunisian Forward and Return pass (see Tunisian Crochet sidebar on page 112), with the rows offset from each other (see Tunisian Staggered Stitch Pattern below). The first row of the pattern begins with a stitch in the space between the *second and third* stitches of the previous row, a stitch in each space across, including the space between the second-to-last and last stitches, and finishes with a stitch in the vertical bar of the last stitch. The following row begins with a stitch in the space between the *first and second* stitches of the previous row, a stitch in each space across, skipping the space between the second-to-last and last stitches, and finishes with a stitch in the vertical bar of the last stitch. When the pattern instructs you to work Tsts in the first space, between the first and 2nd stitches, it is implied that you skip the second-to-last space; and when the pattern instructs you to work Tsts in the 2nd sp, between the 2nd and 3rd stitches, it is implied that you do not skip the second-to-last space.

TUNISIAN STAGGERED STITCH PATT (TSTS PATT)

ROW 1: Tsts in 2nd space (bet 2nd and 3rd sts), Tsts in each space across to end, Tsts in vertical thread of last st. Return.

ROW 2: Tsts in first space (bet 1st and 2nd sts), Tsts in each space across to last space, skip last space, Tsts in vertical thread of last st. Return.

Rep Rows 1 and 2 for patt.

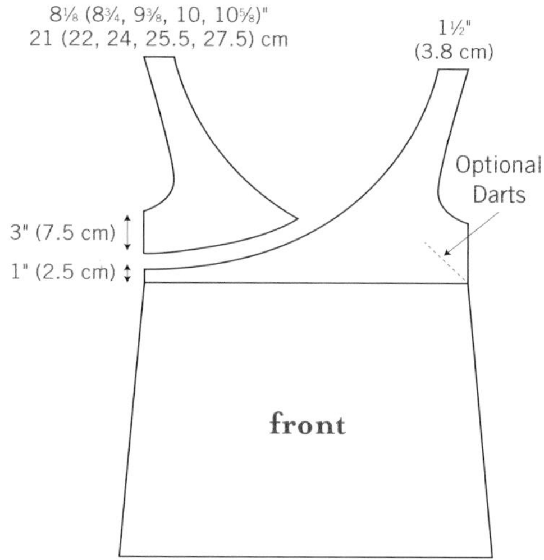

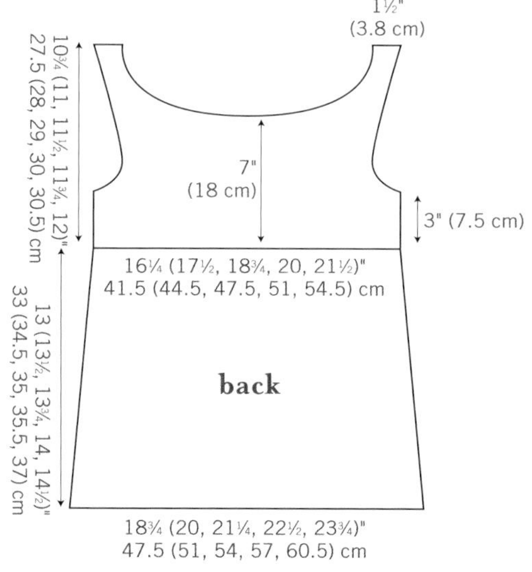

+ PATTERN NOTES +

- For more instruction on Tunisian Crochet, see the sidebar on page 112.
- Be sure to keep a count of your stitches so the edges remain straight.
- When the pattern instructs you to work into a stitch, you will work into the space between the vertical bars.
- To decrease at the end of a forward pass, simply leave the number of stitches to be decreased unworked at the end of the pass, then work the return pass as usual.
- To decrease at the beginning of the forward pass, work a slip stitch in each space for the required number of decreases, following established pattern of alternating where to place the first stitch, then continue with the forward pass as usual.
- To make it easier to follow, read through the pattern and highlight your individual size instructions.

TANK

BACK LOWER WAIST

With standard hook, starting at the waistline and working down, ch 80 (86, 92, 98, 104).

ROW 1: Working through both lps of the ch-1, sc in 2nd ch from hook, *sk 2 ch, sh (see Special Stitches) in next ch, sk 2 ch, sc in next ch; rep from * across, turn—13 (14, 15, 16, 17) shells.

ROW 2: Ch 5 (counts as dc, ch 2 here and throughout), dc in first st, *sc in middle dc of next sh, sh in next sc; rep from * across, ending with (dc, ch 2, dc) in last sc, turn.

ROW 3: Ch 1, sc in first st, *sh in next sc, sc in middle dc of next sh; rep from * across, ending with sc in 3rd ch of beg ch-5, turn.

ROWS 4–9: Repeat Rows 2 and 3.

ROW 10: Ch 5, dc in first st, *sc in middle dc of next sh, sh in next sc; rep from * across, ending with sh in last sc (increase made), turn.

ROW 11: Ch 5, dc in first dc, sc in next dc, sh in next sc, *sc in middle dc of next sh, sh in next sc; rep from * across, ending with sc in 3rd ch of tch, turn.

ROW 12: Ch 5, dc in first sc, *sc in middle dc of next sh, sh in next sc; rep from * across, ending sc in 3rd ch of tch, turn.

ROWS 13–17: Repeat Row 12.

ROW 18: Ch 5, dc in first st, *sc in middle dc of next sh, sh in next sc; rep from * across, ending with sc in 3rd ch of tch, (dtr, ch2, dc through middle of dtr) in same st (increase made), turn.

ROW 19: Ch 5, dc in first st, sk ch-2, sc in next tr, *sh in next sc, sc in middle dc of next sh; rep from * across, ending with sc in 3rd ch of tch, turn.

ROW 20: Ch 5, dc in first st, *sc in middle dc of next sh, sh in next sc; rep from * across, ending with sc in 3rd ch of tch, turn.

ROWS 21–25: Repeat Row 20.

ROWS 26–33: Rep Rows 18–25.

ROWS 34–36: Rep Rows 18–20.

ROWS 37–39 (40, 41, 42, 43): Repeat Row 20.

BODICE

Rotate piece to work into rem bottom lps of the foundation chain. With Tunisian crochet hook, attach yarn to beginning of foundation chain and pick up 78 (84, 90, 96, 102) lps. Return.

Work in Tsts patt (see Special Stitches) until piece measures 3" (7.5 cm) from foundation chain.

ARMHOLE SHAPING

ROW 1: Sl st in first sp, (sl st in next sp) twice, Tsts in each sp across until there are 72 (78, 84, 90, 96) lps on hook. Return.

ROW 2: Sl st in 2nd sp, (sl st in next sp) twice, Tsts in each sp across until there are 66 (72, 78, 84, 90) lps on hook. Return.

ROW 3: Sl st in first sp, sl st in next sp, Tsts in each sp across until there are 62 (68, 74, 80, 86) lps on hook. Return.

ROW 4: Sl st in 2nd sp, Tsts in each sp across until there are 60 (66, 72, 78, 84) lps on hook. Return.

Work even in est patt until piece measures 7" (18 cm) from foundation edge.

BACK RIGHT NECKLINE

ROW 1: Tsts in 2nd sp and each sp across until there are 23 (25, 27, 30, 33) lps on hook. Place stitch marker in stitch at neck edge of this row. Return.

ROW 2: Tsts in first sp and in each sp across until there are 18 (20, 22, 25, 28) lps on hook. Return (5 sts decreased).

Continue in Tsts patt until piece measures 10¾ (11, 11½, 11¾, 12)" (27.5 [28, 29, 30, 30.5] cm) from foundation edge, *at the same time* shape neck edge (end of the forward row) as follows: decrease 5 sts on each of next 1 (1, 1, 1, 1) row, then 2 sts on each of the following 2 (3, 4, 4, 5) rows, then 1 st on each of the following 0 (0, 0, 3, 4) rows. You should have 9 sts for the remainder of strap. Fasten off.

BACK LEFT NECKLINE

ROW 1: From stitch marker, skip 14 (16, 18, 18, 18) spaces, Tsts in each sp across until there are 23 (25, 27, 30, 33) lps on hook. Return.

ROW 2: Sl st in 2nd sp, (sl st in next sp) 4 times, Tsts in each sp to end: 18 (20, 22, 25, 28) lps on hook. Return (5 sts decreased).

Continue in Tsts patt as for first side of the neck, reversing shaping and working decreases at the beginning of the forward row.

FRONT

Work front lower waist same as for Back Lower Waist.

LEFT BODICE

With Tunisian hook and RS facing, attach yarn to beginning of foundation chain and pick up 78 (84, 90, 96, 102) lps. Return.

A/B CUP ONLY, ALL SIZES

ROWS 1–6: Beginning with 2nd row, work even in Tsts patt.

Begin neck shaping as follows:

ROWS 7–10: Continue in est patt, except decrease the neck edge by 5 sts on each of next 2 rows, 3 sts on the following row, and 2 sts on the next row after that.

ROWS 11–13: Continue in est patt, except decrease the neck edge by 1 st for each of the first two rows, then 2 sts on every 3rd row.

Rep Rows 11–13 until piece measures 3" (7.5 cm) from beginning edge for all sizes.

Begin armhole and neck shaping:

Continue to work neck shaping as established in Rows 11–13, *at the same time* decrease the arm edge by 3 sts on each of the next 2 rows, 2 sts on the following row, and 1 st on the row after that.

Armhole shaping is complete. Continue in est patt and continue shaping neck edge as for Rows 11–13 until piece measures 6¼ (6¾, 7½, 8¼, 8¾)" (16 [17, 19, 20.5, 22] cm) from foundation edge. You should have 9 sts remaining.

Work even in est patt on 9 sts until entire piece measures 10¾ (11, 11½, 11¾, 12)" (27.5 [28, 29, 30, 30.5] cm). Fasten off.

C/D CUP ONLY, ALL SIZES

Add darts for C/D cup sizes.

ROWS 1–3: Beginning with 2nd row, work even in Tsts patt.

ROW 4: Tsts in 2nd sp and in each sp across. Return until there are 2 lps rem on hook, continue on to next row.

ROW 5: Tsts in first sp and in each sp across. Return.

ROW 6: Tsts in 2nd sp and in each sp across. Return until there are 5 lps rem on hook.

ROW 7: Tsts in first sp and in each sp across until there are 72 (78, 84, 90, 96) sts on hook. Return.

ROW 8: Tsts in first sp (again) and in each sp across until there are 67 (73, 79, 85, 91) sts on hook. Return until there are 7 lps rem on hook.

ROW 9: Tsts in first sp and in each sp across until there are 64 (70, 76, 82, 88) sts on hook. Return.

ROW 10: Tsts in 2nd sp and in each sp across until there are 62 (68, 74, 80, 86) sts on hook. Return until there are 10 lps rem on hook.

ROW 11: Tsts in first sp and in each sp across until there are 61 (67, 73, 79, 85) sts on hook. Return.

ROW 12: Tsts in first sp (again) and in each sp across until there are 60 (66, 72, 78, 84) sts on hook. Return until there are 12 lps rem on hook.

ROW 13: Tsts in first sp and in each sp across until there are 58 (64, 70, 76, 82) sts on hook. Return.

ROW 14: Tsts in 2nd sp and in each sp across until there are 57 (63, 69, 75, 81) sts on hook. Return until there are 15 lps rem on hook.

ROW 15: Tsts in first sp and in each sp across until there are 56 (62, 68, 74, 80) sts on hook. Return.

ROW 16: Tsts in first sp (again) and in each sp across until there are 54 (60, 66, 72, 78) sts on hook. Return until there are 17 lps rem on hook.

ROW 17: Tsts in first sp and in each sp across across until there are 53 (59, 65, 71, 77) sts on hook. Return.

ROW 18: Tsts in 2nd sp and in each sp across until there are 52 (58, 64, 70, 76) lps on hook. Return until there are 20 lps rem on hook.

ROW 19: Tsts in first sp and in each sp across

until there are 50 (56, 62, 68, 74) lps on hook. Return.

ROW 20: Tsts in first sp (again) and in each sp across until there are 49 (55, 61, 67, 73) lps on hook. Return until there are 22 lps rem on hook.

ROW 21: Tsts in first sp and in each sp across until there are 48 (54, 60, 66, 72) lps on hook. Return.

ROW 22: Tsts in 2nd sp and in each sp across until there are 46 (52, 58, 64, 70) lps on hook. Return.

ROWS 23–25: Continue in Tsts patt, except decrease the neck edge by 1 st for each of the first two rows, then by 2 sts on the third row.

Rep Rows 23–25 two more times.

Begin armhole:

Continue to work neck shaping as established in Rows 23–25, *at the same time* decrease the armhole edge by 3 sts on each of the next two rows, 2 sts on the following row, and 1 st on the row after that.

Armhole shaping is complete. Continue in est patt, shaping neck edge as for Rows 23–25 until piece measures 6¼ (6¾, 7½, 8¼, 8¾)" (16 [17, 19, 21, 22] cm) from beg edge. You should have 9 sts remaining for shoulder strap.

Work evenly in est patt on 9 sts until entire piece measures 10¾ (11, 11½, 11¾, 12)" (27.5 [28, 29, 30, 30.5] cm). Fasten off.

FRONT RIGHT

A/B CUP ONLY, ALL SIZES

Chain 6.

ROW 1: Tsts in 2nd ch from hook and in each ch across until there are 6 lps on hook. Return. Ch 5.

ROW 2: Tsts in 2nd ch from hook and in each ch and sp across until there are 11 lps on hook. Return. Ch 4.

ROW 3: Tsts in 2nd ch from hook and in each ch and sp across until there are 14 lps on hook (sk last sp). Return. Ch 2.

ROW 4: Tsts in 2nd ch from hook and in each sp across until there are 16 lps on hook. Return. Ch 2.

ROW 5: Tsts in 2nd ch from hook and in each sp across until there are 17 lps on hook (sk last sp). Return. Ch 1.

ROW 6: Tsts in first sp and in each sp across until there are 18 lps on hook. Return. Ch 3.

ROW 7: Tsts in 2nd ch from hook and in each ch and sp across until there are 20 lps on hook (sk last sp). Return. Ch 1.

ROW 8: Tsts in first sp and in each sp across until there are 21 lps on hook. Return. Ch 2.

ROW 9: Tsts in 2nd ch from hook and in each sp across until there are 22 lps on hook (sk last sp). Return. Ch 3.

ROW 10: Tsts in 2nd ch from hook and in each ch and sp across until there are 24 lps on hook (sk last sp). Return. Ch 1.

ROW 11: Tsts in first sp and in each sp across until there are 25 lps on hook. Return. Ch 2.

ROW 12: Tsts in 2nd ch from hook and in each sp across until there are 26 lps on hook (sk last sp). Return. Ch 2.

ROW 13: Tsts in 2nd ch from hook and in each sp across until there are 28 lps on hook. Return. Ch 2.

ROW 14: Tsts in 2nd ch from hook and in each sp across until there are 29 lps on hook (sk last sp). Return. Ch 1.

ROW 15: Tsts in first sp and in each sp across until there are 30 lps on hook. Return. Ch 2.

Begin right armhole shaping:

SIZE 28" (71 CM), A/B CUP ONLY

ROW 1: Tsts in 2nd ch from hook, Tsts in first st, in first sp and in each sp across until there are 29 lps on hook. Return. Ch 1.

ROW 2: Pull up a lp in first vertical bar (see Tss in sidebar on page 112; 1 increase made), Tsts in 2nd sp and in each sp across until there are 27 lps on hook. Return.

Beg with Row 2 of Tsts patt, continue to work in pattern, shaping arm and neck edges as follows:

ROW 3: Dec neck edge by 1 st, dec armhole edge by 2 sts. Return.

ROW 4: Dec neck edge by 2 sts, dec armhole edge by 1 st. Return. Tsts.

ROW 5: Dec neck edge by 1 st. Return.

ROW 6: Dec neck edge by 1 st. Return.

ROW 7: Dec neck edge by 2 sts. Return.

ROWS 8–13: Rep Rows 5–7. Return.

Continue to work even in Tsts patt, on rem 9 sts, until piece measures about 10" (25.5 cm) from foundation edge.

SIZE 30" (76 CM), A/B CUP ONLY

ROW 1: Tsts in 2nd ch from hook, in first st, in 2nd sp and in each sp across until there are 29 lps on hook. Return. Ch 1.

ROW 2: Pull up a lp in first vertical bar (see Tss in sidebar on page 112; 1 increase made), Tsts in first sp and in each sp across until there are 27 lps on hook. Return. Ch 1.

ROW 3: Pull up a lp in first vertical bar, Tsts in first st, in 2nd sp and in each sp across until there are 25 lps on hook. Return.

Beg with Row 2 of Tsts patt, continue to work in pattern, shaping neck edge as follows:

ROW 4: Dec neck edge by 1 st. Return.

ROW 5: Dec neck edge by 1 st. Return.

ROW 6: Dec neck edge by 2 sts. Return.

ROWS 7–15: Rep Rows 4–6.

Continue to work even in offset st patt, on rem 9 sts, until piece measures about 10¼" (26 cm) from foundation edge.

SIZE 34" (86.5 CM), A/B CUP ONLY

ROW 1: Tsts in 2nd ch from hook, in first st, in 2nd sp and in each sp across until there are 29 lps on hook. Return. Ch 1.

ROW 2: Pull up a lp in first vertical bar (see Tss in sidebar on page 112; 1 increase made), Tsts in first st, in first sp and in each sp across until there are 27 lps on hook. Return. Ch 1.

ROW 3: Pull up a lp in first vertical bar, Tsts in first st, in 2nd sp and in each sp across until there are 26 lps on hook. Return. Ch 2.

ROW 4: Tsts in 2nd ch from hook, in first st, in

first sp and in each sp across until there are 27 lps on hook. Return. Ch 1.

ROW 5: Pull up a lp in first vertical bar, Tsts in first st, in 2nd sp and in each sp across until there are 28 lps on hook. Return.

Beg with Row 2 of Tsts patt, continue to work in pattern, shaping neck edge as follows:

ROW 6: Dec neck edge by 1 st. Return.

ROW 7: Dec neck edge by 2 sts. Return.

ROW 8: Dec neck edge by 1 st. Return.

ROW 9: Dec neck edge by 1 st. Return.

ROW 10: Dec neck edge by 2 sts. Return.

ROWS 11–19: Rep Rows 8–10.

Continue to work even in Tsts patt, on rem 9 sts, until piece measures about 10¾" (27.5 cm) from foundation edge.

SIZE 36" (91.5 CM), A/B CUP ONLY

ROW 1: Tsts in 2nd ch from hook, in first st, in 2nd sp and in each sp across until there are 29 lps on hook. Return. Ch 1.

ROW 2: Pull up a lp in first vertical bar (see Tss in sidebar on page 112; 1 increase made), Tsts in first st, in first sp and in each sp across until there are 27 lps on hook. Return. Ch 1.

ROW 3: Pull up a lp in first vertical bar, Tsts in first st, in 2nd sp and in each sp across until there are 26 lps on hook. Return. Ch 2.

ROW 4: Tsts in 2nd ch from hook, in first st, in first sp and in each sp across until there are 27 lps on hook. Return. Ch 1.

ROW 5: Pull up a lp in first vertical bar, Tsts in first st, in 2nd sp and in each sp across until there are 28 lps on hook. Return. Ch 1.

ROW 6: Pull up a lp in first vertical bar, Tsts in first st, in first sp and in each sp across until there are 29 lps on hook. Return. Ch 2.

ROW 7: Tsts in 2nd ch from hook, in first st, in 2nd sp and in each sp across until there are 31 lps on hook. Return.

Beg with Row 2 of Tsts patt, continue to work in pattern, shaping neck edge as follows:

ROW 8: Dec neck edge by 2 sts. Return.

ROW 9: Dec neck edge by 1 st. Return.

ROW 10: Dec neck edge by 1 st. Return.

ROW 11: Dec neck edge by 2 sts. Return.

ROWS 12–23: Rep Rows 9–11.

Continue to work even in Tsts patt, on rem 9 sts, until piece measures about 11" (28 cm) from foundation edge.

SIZE 38" (96.5 CM), A/B CUP ONLY

ROW 1: Pull up a lp in first vertical bar (see Tss in sidebar on page 112; 1 increase made), Tsts in first st, in 2nd sp and in each sp across until there are 29 lps on hook. Return. Ch 1.

ROW 2: Pull up a lp in first vertical bar, Tsts in first st, in first sp and in each sp across until there are 27 lps on hook. Return. Ch 1.

ROW 3: Pull up a lp in first vertical bar, Tsts in first st, in 2nd sp and in each sp across until there are 26 lps on hook. Return. Ch 2.

ROW 4. Tsts in 2nd ch from hook, in first st, in first sp and in each sp across until there are 27 lps on hook. Return. Ch 1.

ROW 5. Pull up a lp in first vertical bar, Tsts in first st, in 2nd sp and in each sp across until there are 28 lps on hook. Return. Ch 1.

ROW 6: Pull up a lp in first vertical bar, Tsts in first st, in first sp and in each sp across until there are 29 lps on hook. Return. Ch 2.

ROW 7: Tsts in 2nd ch from hook, in first st, in 2nd sp and in each sp across until there are 31 lps on hook. Return. Ch 1.

ROW 8: Pull up a lp in first vertical bar, Tsts in first st, in first sp and in each sp across until there are 32 lps on hook. Return. Ch 1.

ROW 9: Pull up a lp in first vertical bar, Tsts in first st, in 2nd sp and in each sp across until there are 33 lps on hook. Return.

Beg with Row 2 of Tsts patt, continue to work

in pattern, shaping neck edge as follows:

ROW 10: Dec neck edge by 1 st. Return.

ROW 11: Dec neck edge by 1 st. Return.

ROW 12: Dec neck edge by 2 sts. Return.

ROWS 13–27: Rep Rows 10–12.

Continue to work even in Tsts patt, on rem 9 sts, until piece measures about 11¼" (28.5 cm) from foundation edge.

C/D CUP ONLY, ALL SIZES

Chain 7.

ROWS 1–3: Tsts in 2nd ch from hook and in each ch across until there are 7 lps on hook. Return.

ROW 4: Tsts in first sp and in each sp across until there are 5 lps on hook. Return.

ROW 5: Tsts in 2nd sp and in each sp across until there are 7 lps on hook. Return.

ROW 6: Tsts in first sp and in each sp across. Return.

ROW 7: Tsts in first sp and in each sp across until there are 7 lps on hook (sk 2nd to last sp). Return. Ch 5.

ROW 8: Tsts in 2nd ch from hook and in each ch across until there are 5 lps on hook. Return. Ch 3.

ROW 9: Tsts in 2nd ch from hook, in first st, in 2nd sp and in each sp across until there are 15 lps on hook. Return. Ch 2.

ROW 10: Tsts in 2nd ch from hook, in first st, in first sp and in each sp across until there are 7 lps on hook. Return. Ch 1.

ROW 11: Pull up a lp in first vertical bar (see Tss in sidebar on page 112; 1 increase made), Tsts in first st, in first sp and in each sp across until there are 18 lps on hook (sk 2nd to last sp). Return. Ch 1.

ROW 12: Pull up a lp in first vertical bar, Tsts in first st, in first sp and in each sp across until there are 7 lps on hook. Return. Ch 2.

ROW 13: Tsts in 2nd ch from hook, in first st, in 2nd sp and in each sp across until there are 21 lps on hook. Return. Ch 1.

ROW 14: Pull up a lp in first vertical bar, Tsts in first st, in first sp and in each sp across until there are 7 lps on hook. Return. Ch 1.

ROW 15: Pull up a lp in first vertical bar, Tsts in first st, in first sp and in each sp across until there are 23 lps on hook (sk 2nd to last sp). Return. Ch 2.

ROW 16: Tsts in 2nd ch from hook, in first st, in first sp and in each sp across until there are 8 lps on hook. Return. Ch 1.

ROW 17: Pull up a lp in first vertical bar, Tsts in first st, in 2nd sp and in each sp across until there are 26 lps on hook. Return. Ch 1.

ROW 18: Pull up a lp in first vertical bar, Tsts in first st, in first sp and in each sp across until there are 7 lps on hook. Return. Ch 2.

ROW 19: Tsts in 2nd ch from hook, in first st, in first sp and in each sp across until there are 29 lps on hook (sk 2nd to last sp). Return. Ch 1.

ROW 20: Pull up a lp in first vertical bar, Tsts in first st, in first sp and in each sp across until there are 8 lps on hook. Return. Ch 1.

ROW 21: Pull up a lp in first vertical bar, Tsts in first st, in 2nd sp and in each sp across until there are 31 lps on hook. Return. Ch 2.

ROW 22: Tsts in 2nd ch from hook, in first st, in first sp and in each sp across until there are 33 lps on hook (sk 2nd to last sp). Return. Ch 1.

ROW 23: Pull up a lp in first vertical bar, Tsts in first st, in 2nd sp and in each sp across until there are 34 sts. Return. Ch 1.

ROW 24: Pull up a lp in first vertical bar, Tsts in first st, in first sp and in each sp across until there are 35 sts (sk 2nd to last sp). Return. Ch 2.

ROW 25: Tsts in 2nd ch from hook, in first st, in 2nd sp and in each sp across until there are 37 sts. Return. Ch 1.

ROW 26: Pull up a lp in first vertical bar, Tsts

in first st, in first sp and in each sp across until there are 38 sts (sk 2nd to last sp). Return. Ch 1.

ROW 27: Pull up a lp in first vertical bar, Tsts in first st, in 2nd sp and in each sp across until there are 39 sts. Return.

Size 28" (71 cm) only: Skip to Arm and Neck Shaping. For larger sizes, continue to next row.

ROW 28: Ch 2, Tsts in 2nd ch from hook and in each sp across until there are 41 lps on hook. Return. Ch 1.

ROW 29: Pull up a lp in first vertical bar, Tsts in first st, in first sp and in each sp across until there are 42 lps on hook. Return. Ch 1.

Size 30" (76 cm) only: Skip to Arm and Neck Shaping. For larger sizes, continue to next row.

ROW 30: Pull up a lp in first vertical bar, Tsts in first st, in first sp and in each sp across until there are 43 lps on hook. Return. Ch 2.

ROW 31: Tsts in 2nd ch from hook and in each sp across until there are 45 lps on hook. Return.

Begin armhole and neck shaping:

SIZE 28" (71 CM), C/D CUP ONLY

Beg with Row 2 of Tsts patt, continue to work in pattern, shaping neck edge as follows:

ROW 1: Dec neck edge by 1 st. Return.

ROW 2: Dec neck edge by 1 st. Return.

ROW 3: Dec neck edge by 2 sts. Return.

ROW 4: Rep Row 28.

ROW 5: Dec neck edge by 1 st, dec armhole edge by 3 sts. Return.

ROW 6: Dec neck edge by 2 sts, dec armhole edge by 3 sts. Return.

ROW 7: Dec neck edge by 1 st, dec armhole edge by 2 sts. Return.

ROW 8: Dec neck edge by 1 st, dec armhole edge by 1 st. Return.

ROW 9: Dec neck edge by 2 sts, dec armhole edge by 1 st. Return.

ROWS 10–15. Rep Rows 1-3 two more times.

Continue to work even in Tsts patt, on rem 9 sts, until piece measures about 10" (25.5 cm) from foundation edge.

SIZE 30" (76 CM) C/D CUP ONLY

ROW 1: Pull up a lp in first vertical bar (see Tss in sidebar on page 112; 1 increase made), Tsts in first st, in first sp and in each sp across until there are 43 lps on hook. Return. Ch 1.

ROW 2: Sl st in 2nd sp, Tsts in next sp and in each sp across until there are 42 lps on hook. Return.

Beg with Row 2 of Tsts patt, continue to work in pattern, shaping arm and neck edges as follows:

ROWS 3–4: Dec neck edge by 1 st, dec armhole edge by 3 sts. Return.

ROW 5: Dec neck edge by 2 sts, dec armhole edge by 2 sts. Return.

ROW 6: Dec neck edge by 1 st, dec armhole edge by 1 st. Return.

ROW 7: Dec neck edge by 1 st. Return.

ROW 8: Dec neck edge by 2 sts. Return.

ROW 9: Dec neck edge by 1 st. Return.

ROW 10: Dec neck edge by 1 st. Return.

ROW 11: Dec neck edge by 2 sts. Return.

ROWS 12–20: Rep Rows 9–11.

Continue to work even in Tsts patt, on rem 9 sts, until piece measures about 10¼" (26 cm) from foundation edge.

SIZE 34" (86.5 CM), C/D CUP ONLY

Beg with Row 2 of Tsts patt, continue to work in pattern, shaping arm and neck edges as follows:

ROWS 1–2: Dec neck edge by 1 st, dec armhole edge by 3 sts. Return.

ROW 3: Dec neck edge by 2 sts, dec armhole edge by 2 sts. Return.

ROW 4: Dec neck edge by 1 st, dec armhole edge by 1 st. Return.

ROW 5: Dec neck edge by 1 st. Return.

ROW 6: Dec neck edge by 2 sts. Return.

ROW 7: Dec neck edge by 1 st. Return.

ROW 8: Dec neck edge by 1 st. Return.

ROW 9: Dec neck edge by 2 sts. Return.

ROWS 10–21: Rep Rows 7–9.

Continue to work even in Tsts patt, on rem 9 sts, until piece measures about 10¾" (27.5 cm) from foundation edge.

SIZE 36" (91.5 CM), C/D CUP ONLY

ROW 1: Ch 1, Pull up a lp in first vertical bar (see Tss in sidebar on page 112; 1 increase made), Tsts in first st, in first sp and in each sp across until there are 43 lps on hook. Return. Ch 1.

ROW 2: Pull up a lp in first vertical bar, Tsts in first st, in first sp and in each sp across until there are 41 lps on hook. Return.

Continue to work in Tsts patt, shaping arm and neck edges as follows:

ROW 3. Dec neck edge by 1 st, dec armhole edge by 2 sts. Return.

ROW 4: Dec neck edge by 2 st, dec armhole edge by 1 sts. Return.

ROW 5: Dec neck edge by 1 st. Return.

ROW 6: Dec neck edge by 1 st. Return.

ROW 7: Dec neck edge by 2 sts. Return.

ROWS 8–24: Rep Rows 5–7 five more times. Rep Rows 5-6 once more.

Continue to work even in Tsts patt, on rem 9 sts, until piece measures about 11" (28 cm) from foundation edge.

SIZE 38" (96.5 CM), C/D CUP ONLY

ROW 1: Ch 1, pull up a lp in first vertical bar (see Tss in sidebar on page 112; 1 increase made), Tsts in first st, in first sp and in each sp across until there are 43 lps on hook. Return. Ch 1.

ROW 2: Pull up a lp in first vertical bar, Tsts in first st, in first sp and in each sp across until there are 41 lps on hook. Return. Ch 2.

ROW 3: Tsts in 2nd ch from hook and in each sp across until there are 41 lps on hook. Return. Ch 1.

ROW 4: Pull up a lp in first vertical bar, Tsts in first st, in first sp and in each sp across until there are 41 lps on hook. Return. Ch 1.

ROW 5: Pull up a lp in first vertical bar, Tsts in first st, in first sp and in each sp across until there are 42 lps on hook. Return.

ROW 6: Sl st in first sp, Tsts in next sp and in each sp across until there are 41 lps on hook. Return.

Continue to work in Tsts patt, shaping neck edges as follows:

ROW 7: Dec neck edge by 1 st. Return.

ROW 8: Dec neck edge by 1 st. Return.

ROW 9: Dec neck edge by 2 sts. Return.

ROWS 10–20: Rep Rows 7–9 seven more times.

Continue to work even in Tsts patt, on rem 9 sts, until piece measures about 11¼" (28.5 cm) from foundation edge.

FINISHING

Sew a button to the 1" (3 cm) end of the large front piece. Weave in ends. Block all three pieces (see Block It sidebar on page 66).

Measure the width of the large front piece of the tank. Place a stitch marker at the end of the row that hits the halfway mark on the neckline. Match the stitch marker on the front pieces together. Sew together at shoulders, down sides, and across the front. Try the cami on to make sure it fits right. If either side is uneven, you can add or remove shoulder strap rows to adjust.

Recommended for A/B cups: Sew an invisible zipper into one side seam, from the armhole down 3–4" (7.5–10 cm). The Tunisian stitch doesn't stretch very well, and a zipper may make the finished garment easier to put on and take off.

Sc evenly around armholes and necklines if desired. This is a good place to make sure the top fits correctly. You can make even decreases along the neckline if it doesn't lay flat against your chest.

designer in profile

megan granholm

PHOTO BY CORY GRANHOLM

Megan grew up outside Portland, Oregon, where she used to pretend the mimosa tree in her yard was a horse. In her words, she was a perfect child who translated her nose-picking prowess into *mad skillz* with her crochet hook. Now she's an accountant and rushes home from work to get in some quality time with her creativity.

Megan started writing crochet patterns for her own use so she could repeat the design later. Her first published pattern—a lace cowl—appeared in the Fall 2005 issue of CrochetMe.com. She was introduced to CrochetMe.com in another online community, and was an avid reader before she became a contributor to the site. She's a lover of natural fibers and a lefty who learned to crochet by pretending she was looking in a mirror and going backwards.

In her words: "One of my favorite things about crocheting is that once you get to know how to make the stitches and you're pretty aware of how garments are constructed, you can dive off into the deep end and at the very least make all kinds of alterations (if you don't feel like writing up a pattern of your own). If I can't quite get something to fit my body shape exactly, I can decrease or increase a couple of rows. If I don't like a stitch pattern, I can substitute another. It's vital to creativity to keep delving into and stretching your own design skills and altering patterns is a great way to start."

YOU CAN KEEP TRACK OF MEGAN AT HER BLOG LOOPDEDOO.BLOGSPOT.COM.

technically speaking: TUNISIAN CROCHET

One of my favorite crochet variations is Tunisian, or Afghan, crochet (the names are used interchangeably). I've heard this technique described as a hybrid of knitting and crochet, but that's not entirely accurate. Each row of Tunisian crochet involves both picking up and binding off all the stitches in that row. Because all the stitches in a given row are involved, you need to use a long hook, called a Tunisian crochet hook or Afghan hook. With a hook on one end, the shaft is about 14" (36 cm) long, just like a knitting needle. The length of the shaft accommodates all the stitches you pick up in each row.

Because each row consists of picking up and binding off, the first step in stitching a row is called the *forward pass* and the second step is called the *return pass*. A nifty thing about Tunisian crochet is that you don't turn your work. You simply go from one end of your work to the other, picking up stitches, then you work back, binding them off.

The many varied Tunisian crochet stitches create textures different from those of regular crochet stitches, but I'll only cover two here: *Tunisian simple stitch* (Tss), which is the basic stitch, and the stitch that's used in the Megan Granholm's Five O'Clock Tank pattern (page 98), which she and I call *Tunisian staggered stitch* (Tsts). A slight variation on Tunisian simple stitch, Tunisian staggered stitch offsets one row of stitches from another, hence its name.

Note: Tunisian crochet involves the equivalent of a turning chain of one at the end of the forward pass, even though the work isn't turned.

TUNISIAN SIMPLE STITCH (TSS)

Make a foundation chain equal to the required number of stitches.

FOUNDATION FORWARD PASS: Insert hook in 2nd ch from hk and pull up a lp, *insert hook in next ch and pull up a lp, rep from * to the end (Figure 1).

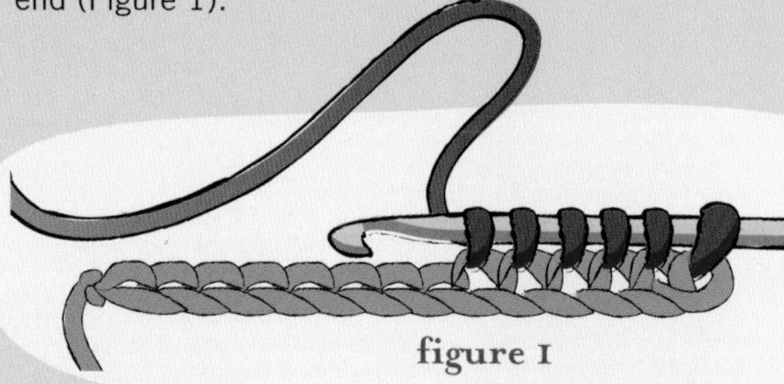

figure 1

RETURN PASS: Ch 1, *yo, pull through first 2 lps on hook, rep from * to end (one lp remains on hook—this st counts as the first st of the next row) (Figure 2).

Notice that the stitches resemble squares. We refer to the vertical bars as *vertical bars* and to the horizontal bars between them as *horizontal bars*.

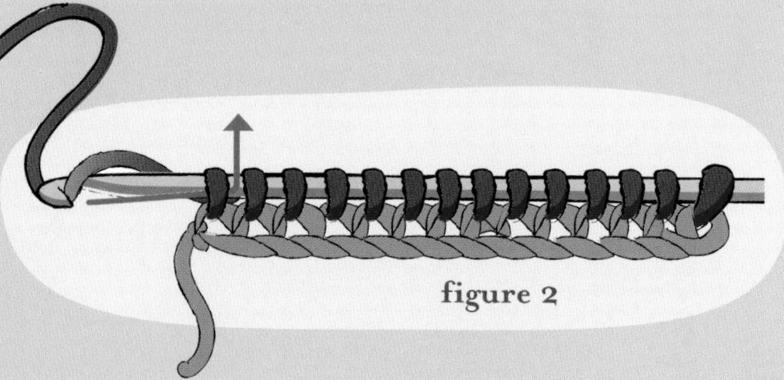

figure 2

ROW 2, FORWARD PASS: Insert hook under the 2nd vertical bar and pull up a lp (Figure 3), *insert hook under next vertical bar and pull up a lp, rep from * to last st, insert hook under both vertical lps at the end of the row, pull up a lp.

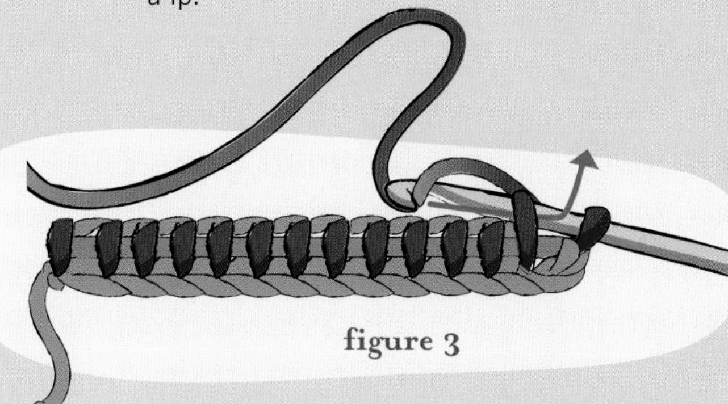

figure 3

RETURN PASS: Ch 1, *yo, pull through first 2 lps on hook, rep from * to end (one lp remains on hook—this counts as the first st of the next row).

Repeat Row 2.

At the end of your work, do a proper Tunisian crochet bind-off row for a firmer edge. To do so, pick up and bind off during the forward pass alone: Insert hook under 2nd vertical bar and pull up a lp, yo and pull through 2 lps on hook, *insert hook under next vertical bar and pull up a lp, yo and pull through 2 lps on hook*, rep from * to * to the end of the row (1 lp remains on the hook). Fasten off.

TUNISIAN STAGGERED STITCH (TSTS)

To work the Tsts that's used in the Five O'Clock Tank, work the Foundation row as for Tss. The following rows involve inserting your hook under the horizontal spaces between the vertical bars. You'll alternate rows of skipping the first and last stitches of the row to create the staggered effect.

ROW 2, FORWARD PASS: Insert hook under the horizontal bars bet the 2nd and 3rd sts from the prev row and pull up a lp, *insert hook under the horizontal bars bet the next 2 sts and pull up a lp*, rep from * to * to end, insert hook into last st as for Tss and pull up a lp.

RETURN PASS: As for Tss.

ROW 3, FORWARD PASS: Insert hook under the horizontal bars bet the 1st and 2nd sts from the prev row and pull up a lp, *insert hook under the horizontal bars bet the next 2 sts and pull up a lp*, rep from * to * to end, skipping sp between last 2 sts, insert hook into last st as for Tss and pull up a lp.

RETURN PASS: As for Tss.

Rep Rows 2 and 3.

cocoon *bag*

Cecily Keim

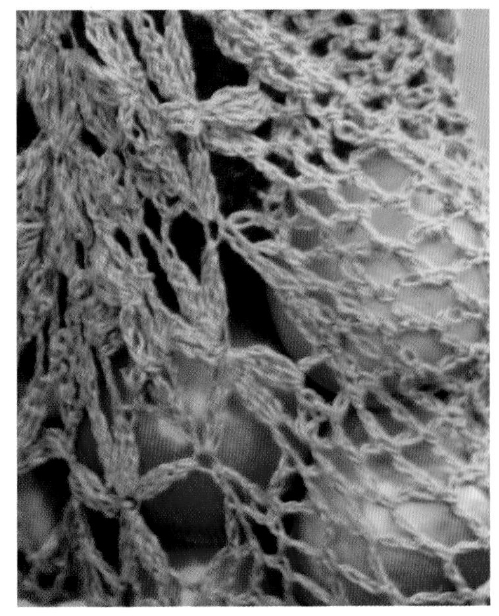

concentration rating 1 2 3 **4**

CECILY'S INSPIRATION

Visits to my neighborhood farmer's market have been a huge source of inspiration in my life. I have a collection of bland mesh and canvas bags for my weekly market visit, but I wanted a bag that would look as unique and pretty as I feel when I walk home with arms full of flowers and fresh fruit. The hemp yarn gave me room to play with the mesh structure, so I came up with this ruffled, crumpled, cocoon-like texture that most yarns won't hold. I like playing with flower patterns by trying new ways of chopping up the rows to see how the flower pattern looks with different textures in between the flower rows. In this bag, I love how the flower rows are stiff and the mesh rows just explode from them.

FINISHED SIZE

15" (38 cm) tall and 10" (25.5 cm) wide.

YARN

Lana Knits, All Hemp 3 (100% hemp; 165 yd [150 m]/50 g), sapphire, 3 skeins.

SUBSTITUTION: About 495 yd (453 m) of strong fingering-weight (Super Fine #1) yarn.

HOOK

Size G/7 (4.5 mm). Change hook size if necessary to obtain the correct gauge.

NOTIONS

Yarn needle.

GAUGE

One flower from Rows 5 and 6 = 2½" (6.5 cm).

+ SPECIAL STITCHES +

EXTENDED TREBLE CROCHET (ETR): Yo twice, insert hook in next st, yo and pull up a lp, yo and pull through the first lp on the hook, [yarn over and draw the yarn through 2 lps on hook] 3 times.

2 EXTENDED TREBLE CROCHET CLUSTER (ETR2CL): Work 1 etr to the last step (2 lps on hook), in the next st, work a 2nd etr to the last step (3 lps on hook), yarn over and pull through all lps on hook.

3 EXTENDED TREBLE CROCHET CLUSTER (ETR3CL): Work 1 etr to the last step (2 lps on hook), in the same st work a 2nd etr to the last step (3 lps on hook), in the same st work a 3rd etr to the last step (4 lps on hook), yarn over and pull through all lps on the hook.

5 EXTENDED TREBLE CROCHET CLUSTER (ETR5CL) [WORKED OVER SEVERAL STS]: Work 5 etr as directed, working each etr to the last step, yo and pull through all lps on hook.

8 EXTENDED TREBLE CROCHET CLUSTER (ETR8CL) [WORKED OVER SEVERAL STS]: Work 8 etr as directed, working each etr to the last step, yo and pull through all lps on hook.

+ PATTERN NOTES +

- When directed to work in the top of a treble crochet cluster, work into the space that forms the center of the flower.

BAG

Ch 130.

ROW 1: Sc in 2nd ch from hook, *ch 3, sk 3 chs, sc in next ch; rep from * across turn.

ROW 2: Ch 1, sc in first sc, ch 3, sk first ch-3 sp, (etr3cl [see Special Stitches], ch 6, etr3cl) in next sc, ch 3, sc in next sc, *ch 3, (etr3cl, ch 6, etr3cl) in next sc, ch 3, sc in next sc; rep from * across, turn.

ROW 3: *Ch 3, sc in next ch-3 sp, [ch 3, sc] in ch-6 sp 4 times, ch 3, sc in next ch-3 sp, ch 3, sc in next sc; rep from * across, turn.

ROW 4: Ch 3, sc in first ch-3 sp, *ch 3, sc in next ch-3 sp; rep from * across, turn.

ROW 5: Ch 5, sk first ch-3 sp, etr3cl in next sc, ch 5, etr2cl (see Special Stitches) in 5th ch from hook, sk 2 ch-3 sps, sc in next sc, *ch 5, etr8cl (see Special Stitches) worked as follows: (2 etr in 5th ch from hook, sk 2 ch-3 sps, 3 etr in next sc, sk 3 ch-3 sps, 3 etr in next sc), ch 5, etr2cl in 5th ch from hook, sk 2 ch-3 sps, sc in next sc; rep from * until 4 ch-3 sps remain, ch 5, etr5cl (see Special Stitches) worked as follows: (2 etr in 5th ch from hook, sk 3 ch-3 sps, 3 etr in last ch-3 sp), turn.

ROW 6: Ch 5, etr2cl in 5th ch from hook, ch 4, sc in sc between flower groups from the prev row, *ch 3, (etr3cl, ch 6, etr3cl) in top of next etr8cl (sp at center of flower), ch 3, sc in sc between flower groups from the prev row; rep from * across row to half flower at end of row, ch 4, etr3cl in top of etr3cl from the beginning of the prev row (sp at center of half flower), turn.

ROW 7: Ch 3, sc in first ch-4 sp, ch 3, sc in next sc, *ch 3, sc in next ch-3 sp, [ch 3, sc] in ch-6 sp 4 times, ch 3, sc in next ch-3 sp, ch 3, sc in next sc; rep from * to half flower at end of row, ch 3, sc in ch-4 sp, ch 3, sl st in top of etr2cl (petal) from previous row, turn.

ROWS 8–12: Rep Row 4.

ROW 13: Ch 5, sc in first ch-3 sp, *ch 5, sc in next ch-3 sp; rep from * across, turn.

ROW 14: Ch 5, sc in first ch-5 sp, *ch 5, sc in next ch-5 sp; rep from * across, turn.

ROW 15: Ch 3, sc in first ch-5 sp, *ch 3, sc in next ch-3 sp; rep from * across, turn.

ROWS 16–17: Rep Row 4.

ROW 18: Ch 8, etr8cl worked as follows: (2 etr in 5th ch from hook, 3 etr in first ch-3 sp, sk next ch-3 sp, 3 etr in next ch-3 sp), ch 5, etr2cl in 5th ch from hook, sk 2 ch-3 sps, *sc in next sc, ch 5, etr8cl worked as follows: (2 etr in 5th ch from hook, sk 2 ch-3 sps, 3 etr in next ch-3 sp, sk 1 ch-3 sp, 3 etr in next ch-3 sp), ch 5, etr2cl in 5th ch from hook, sk 2 ch-3 sps; rep from * across, sc in next sc, etr in last ch-3 sp of previous row, turn.

ROW 19: *Ch 3, (etr3cl, ch 6, etr3cl) in top of next etr8cl, ch 3, sc in sc between flower groups from prev row, rep from * across, ending with sc in 5th ch of tch from prev row, turn.

ROW 20: Rep Row 3.

ROW 21: Rep Row 4.

ROW 22: Rep Row 5.

ROW 23: Ch 1, sc in top of first etr5cl, *ch 3, sc in next sc, ch 3, sc in top of next etr8cl; rep from * across ending with sc in top of last etr3cl. Fasten off.

FINISHING

Weave in yarn ends. Hand wash, roll in a towel to soak up excess moisture, place on dry towels and shape the fabric so that the flower rows are neat and straight, and the mesh rows are buckled. Let dry overnight if necessary. (See Block It sidebar on page 66.)

Fold lengthwise and seam along each side.

STRAP

Use your finger or a larger hook to chain several strands to your preferred length. Attach strap at sides.

variations *baskets*

Carol Ventura

concentration rating 1 **2** 3 4

CAROL'S INSPIRATION

Many of my pieces are inspired by other cultures. I often rework patterns from Native American baskets, Islamic tiles, African gourds, Maori beadwork and a variety of other sources. The triangle-stripe motif on these baskets is actually based on a design engraved in a knife on exhibit in an ethnographic museum in Belgium. The flared shape of the baskets is similar to vessels from ancient Mesopotamia. I can't help it—I'm an art historian. I love to visit museums and can't help being inspired by their fabulous collections!

FINISHED SIZE

BEFORE FELTING:
Small basket: 6¼" (16 cm) high, 7⅝" (19.5 cm) diameter, 24" (61 cm) circumference. *Medium basket:* 14¼" (36 cm) high, 14" (35.5 cm) diameter, 44" (112 cm) circumference. *Large basket (page 120):* 23" (58.5 cm) high, 23" (58.5 cm) diameter, 72" (183 cm) circumference.

AFTER FELTING:
Small basket: 5" (12.5 cm) high, 5" (12.5 cm) diameter, 16" (40.5 cm) circumference. *Medium basket:* 12" (30.5 cm) high, 9⅞" (25.5 cm) diameter, 31" (78.5 cm) circumference. *Large basket (page 120):* 19" (48.5 cm) high, 16½" (42 cm) diameter, 52" (132 cm) circumference.

YARN

Brown Sheep Burly Spun (100% wool; 132 yd [121 m]/8 oz). *Small basket:* #BS38 lotus pink (MC), ⅓ skein; #BS120 limeade (CC1), ⅓ skein. *Medium basket:* #BS10 cream (MC), 1⅓ skeins; #BS110 orange you glad (CC1), ½ skein; #BS120 limeade (CC2), ⅔ skein. *Large basket (page 120):* #BS 155 lemon drop (MC), 3 skeins; #BS79 blue boy (CC1), 1 skein; #BS38 lotus pink (CC2), 1 skein; #BS110 orange you glad (CC3), 1 1/10 skeins.

SUBSTITUTIONS: Bulky-weight (Super Bulky #6) 100% wool (not superwash). *Small basket:* 50 yd (46 m) each MC and CC1. *Medium basket:* 175 yd (160 m) MC, 75 yd (66 m) CC1, 100 yds (91 m) CC2. *Large basket (page 120):* 400 yd (366 m) MC, 150 yd (138 m) each of CC1, CC2, and CC3.

HOOK

Size Q (16 mm). Change hook size if necessary to obtain the correct gauge.

NOTIONS

Stitch marker, yarn needle.

GAUGE

7 sc and 7 sc rows = 4" (10 cm) before felting.

+ PATTERN NOTES +

- With tapestry crochet, one yarn is single crocheted while another is carried (see Tapestry Crochet sidebar on page 122).
- This project is worked as a spiral, not in concentric rings, so DO NOT JOIN at the end of each round. To keep track of where each round ends, slip a stitch marker into the top of the last stitch of the round. Remove the marker to work the last stitch and slip it into the new last stitch at the end of each round.
- The motif is 6 stitches wide at the bottom, and since every row of the base is a multiple of 6, you can size your basket to meet your needs. Once crocheted, put them in the washing machine and watch them magically shrink and felt. The beauty of felted tapestry crochet is the fabric is thick and the pattern is visible on both sides.

large

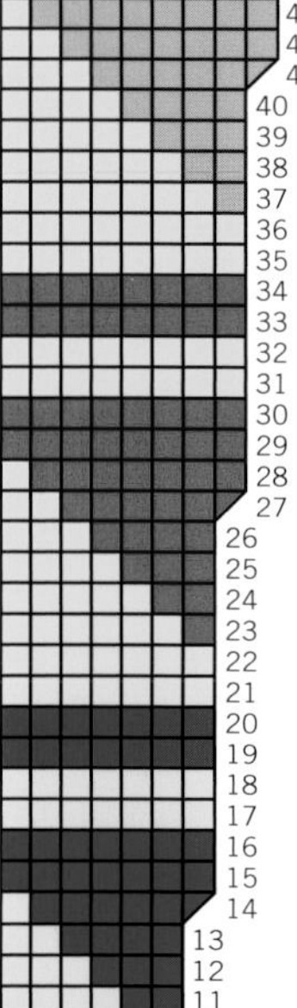

medium

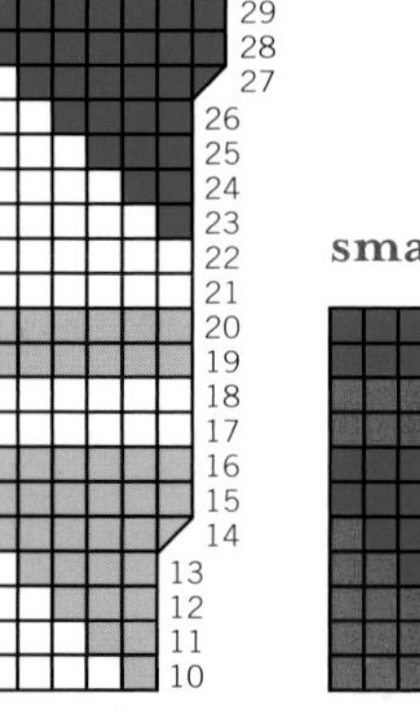

small

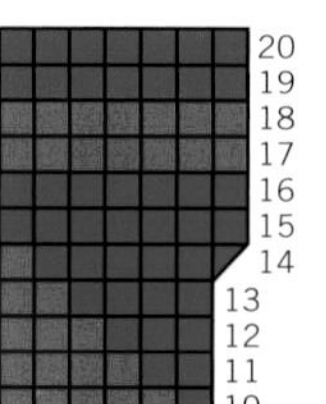

BASKET

ALL SIZES

With MC, and leaving a 6" (15 cm) tail, ch 4, sl st in first ch to form a ring.

RND 1: Sc 6 sts loosely into ring (while carrying MC tail).

RND 2: Start to carry CC1 (see sidebar on page 122). With MC work 2 sc in each st around—12 sts.

RND 3: 2 sc in each st around—24 sts.

RND 4: * Sc in next st, 2 sc in next st, rep from * around—36 sc.

SMALL BASKET: Skip to Rnd 10.

RND 5: Sc in each st around.

RND 6: * Sc in each of next 2 sts, 2 sc in next st, rep from * around—48 sc.

RND 7: * Sc in each of next 3 sts, 2 sc in next st, rep from * around—60 sc.

MEDIUM BASKET: Skip to Rnd 10.

RND 8: * Sc in each of next 4 sts, 2 sc in next st, rep from * around—72 sc.

RND 9: * Sc in each of next 5 sts, 2 sc in next st, rep from * around—84 sc.

BEGIN TAPESTRY CROCHET MOTIF

RND 10: *Carrying unused yarn, with CC1 sc in next st (see sidebar page 122), with MC sc in each of next 5 sts; rep from * around.

RND 11: *With CC1 sc in each of next 2 sts, with MC sc in each of next 4 sts; rep from * around.

RND 12: *With CC1 sc in each of next 3 sts, with MC sc in each of next 3 sts; rep from * around.

RND 13: * With CC1 sc in each of next 4 sts, with MC sc in each of next 2 sts; rep from * around.

RND 14: *With CC1 work 2 sc in next st, sc in each of next 4 sts, with MC sc in next st; rep from * around.

RNDS 15–20: Continue in tapestry sc, working 2 rows in CC1, 2 rows in MC, then 2 rows in CC1.

SMALL BASKET: Sl st in next st with CC1. Fasten off.

RND 21: While carrying CC1, sc in each st around with MC, then cut CC1.

RND 22: Begin to carry CC2, then sc in each st around with MC.

RND 23: *With CC2 sc in next st, with MC sc in each of next 6 sts; rep from * around.

RND 24: *With CC2 sc in each of next 2 sts, with MC sc in each of next 5 sts; rep from * around.

RND 25: *With CC2 sc in each of next 3 sts, with MC sc in each of next 4 sts; rep from * around.

RND 26: *With CC2 sc in each of next 4 sts, with MC sc in each of next 3 sts; rep from * around.

RND 27: *With CC2 work 2 sc next st, sc in each of next 4 sts, with MC sc in each of next 2 sts; rep from * around.

RND 28: *With CC2 sc in each of next 7 sts, with MC sc in next st; rep from * around.

RNDS 29–34: Continue in tapestry sc, working 2 rows in CC2, 2 rows in MC, then 2 rows in CC2.

MEDIUM BASKET: Sl st in next st with CC2. Fasten off.

RND 35: While carrying CC2, sc in each st around with MC, then cut CC2.

RND 36: Begin to carry CC3, sc in each st around with MC.

RND 37: *With CC3 sc in next st, with MC sc in each of next 7 sts; rep from * around.

RND 38: *With CC3 sc in each of next 2 sts, with MC sc in each of next 6 sts; rep from * around.

RND 39: *With CC3 sc in each of next 3 sts, with MC sc in each of next 5 sts; rep from * around.

RND 40: * With CC3 sc in each of next 4 sts, with MC sc in each of next 4 sts; rep from * around.

RND 41: * With CC3 work 2 sc in next st, sc in each of next 4 sts, with MC sc in each of next 3 sts; rep from * around.

RND 42: * With CC3 sc in each of next 7 sts, with MC sc in each of next 2 sts; rep from * around.

RND 43: * With CC3 sc in each of next 8 sts, with MC sc in next st; rep from * around.

RNDS 44–49: Continue in tapestry sc, working 2 rows in CC3, 2 rows in MC, then 2 rows in CC3.

Sl st in next st with CC3. Fasten off.

FINISHING

Weave in yarn ends. To felt, set the washing machine for hot wash, cold rinse, and normal agitation. Wash the Small Basket 5 times (Medium 6 times; Large 8 times) with mild soap (Ivory Dishwashing Liquid works great). The baskets will shrink a little each time they are washed. Steam-iron baskets into shape right out of the washing machine, allow to air-dry, then steam-iron one more time. Because the felted fabric is so thick, allow a day or two for the baskets to dry completely.

technically speaking: TAPESTRY CROCHET

If you've been around the crochet world, you might already consider Carol Ventura to be synonymous with tapestry crochet. Her favorite technique is used worldwide to do color work in crochet with an effect similar to Fair Isle knitting (without the pesky stranding) and intarsia.

figure 1

figure 2

To work tapestry crochet in the round is quite simple. Begin as you normally would with your main color yarn (MC). When directed in the pattern, begin to carry the contrast color yarn (CC) as follows:

Leaving a 6" (15 cm) tail, work your next st in the MC while laying the CC strand over the st. This technique is the same one you might use to crochet over a yarn tail to hide it in your work. Continue to crochet the MC over the CC color (Figure 1).

Then, when you're directed to switch colors, do the following:

Work the next st in the MC until two lps remain on your hook, then draw the CC yarn through the two lps, dropping the MC (Figure 2). Continue crocheting the CC yarn over the MC yarn to hide the latter until you need it again (Figure 3). Do not carry more than one color at a time.

To keep the design looking seamless, you don't join each round with slip stitch when you work in tapestry crochet. Use a marker to indicate the last stitch of the round and work in a spiral.

Read color charts beginning in the bottom right-hand corner. Read each row of the chart from right to left. When you work in rows instead of rounds, follow odd rows from right to left and even rows from left to right. Because you don't turn your work when you do tapestry crochet in the round, you read every row of a chart from right to left. For lefties, instead of rewriting instructions to make them more useful to you, photocopy the color and stitch charts and flip them to change their orientation.

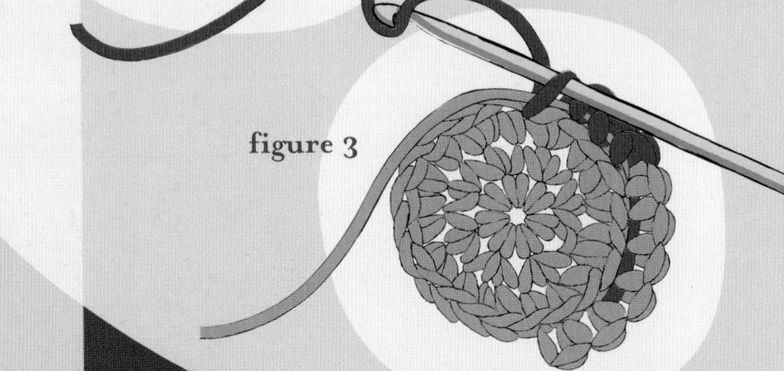

figure 3

PHOTO BY PATTY HAAG

designer in profile

carol ventura

Carol is a big fan of endorphins. Whether we know it or not we're all a big fan of endorphins, really, since they're the handy biochemicals that make us feel good. She says, "Repetitive activities (such as tapestry crochet), sex, and eating chocolate release endorphins. The great thing about tapestry crochet, though, is it doesn't transmit communicable diseases, it doesn't make you gain weight or give you pimples, and when you're finished, you have a great project to brag about!" And there's simply no denying that.

Carol is a professor of art history and her work in tapestry crochet has appeared in many publications including her own books. A designer of items from the simplest small baskets to elaborate tapestry portraits, Carol's priority is to educate.

When she made her first submission to CrochetMe.com, I was surprised. I'd seen her work in print magazines and didn't know if I'd scare her away by telling her we didn't have a budget to pay for designs. She replied that she didn't mind at all—it was her goal to reach as many people as possible to teach them about her favorite technique. And teach she does. From casual readers who have never tried color work before to the scores of crocheters who attend her classes yearly, people all over the world have benefited from Carol's clear and thorough instructions and her generosity with information.

Carol was a Navy brat, moving from town to town when she was growing up. She first encountered tapestry crochet in the late 1970s during her time as a Peace Corps volunteer in Guatemala. After returning to the United States, she unraveled one of the bags she brought home with her, and discovered the techniques she has been teaching and using ever since.

Carol has several art degrees and has taught ceramics, printmaking, jewelry design, photography, and several fiber arts at the college level. Her crochet art hasn't gotten as much attention in crochet publications as her more functional designs, but check out her website to see her gallery work. As Carol puts it, "My latest pieces, which look like religious icons, are feminist because they show Mary teaching Jesus (instead of the other way around). Although I was taught that Jesus was born knowing everything, I believe that his mother taught him a lot. Obviously, attending Catholic school in my 'formative years' and living in the Bible Belt continue to influence my work. Tapestry crochet is very therapeutic for me. I deal with issues and get endorphins at the same time—a win-win."

READ MORE ABOUT CAROL'S WORK AT TAPESTRYCROCHET.COM WHERE YOU'LL ALSO FIND LINKS TO TUTORIALS.

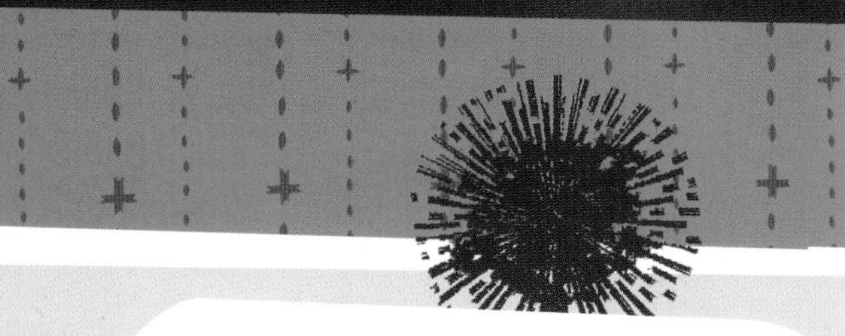

circle *rug*

Donna Hulka

concentration rating 1 **2** 3 4

DONNA'S INSPIRATION

I've always loved circles, but I wasn't wild about crocheting them until I discovered the adjustable ring (see sidebar on page 130). It allows the center hole to be pulled tightly closed. Now I've gone circle crazy and this rug is one of the happy results. I always have idea seeds tucked away here and there in my thoughts; it just takes the right motivation to make them sprout. After I settled on creating a circle motif rug, one of the most exciting parts began—thinking about and experimenting with the design, taking what was in my head and making it reality. From the idea to the utterly decadent box of wool yarn on my doorstep to the rug that beckons me to stand on it, this design has been, as they all are, a wonderful adventure.

FINISHED SIZE

Wool version (at left): 25" (63.5 cm) wide and 35" (89 cm) long. *Acrylic version (page 129):* 23" (58.5 cm) wide and 31½" (80 cm) long.

YARN

Wool version (at left): Halcyon Rug Wool (100% wool; 65 yd [59 m]/4 oz): color #157 (MC), 6 skeins; color #155 (CC), 1 skein; color #154 (CC1), 1 skein; color 107 (CC2), 2 skeins. *Acrylic version (page 129):* Red Heart Super Saver (100% acrylic; 364 yd [333 m]/7 oz): #382 country blue (MC), 2 skeins; #360 cafe (CC), ⅓ skein; #330 linen (CC1), ⅓ skein; #365 coffee (CC2), ⅔ skein. Red Heart yarn distributed by Coats and Clark.

HOOK

Size M or N/13 (9 mm) and size N or P/15 (10 mm). Change hook size if necessary to obtain the correct gauge.

NOTIONS

Yarn needle, stitch markers, small amount of masking tape.

GAUGE

Circle motif for wool version: 3⅝" (9.5 cm) diameter with smaller hook. *Circle motif for acrylic version:* 3½" (9 cm) diameter with smaller hook.

Gauge is not essential in this pattern.

+ SPECIAL STITCHES +

JOINING SLIP STITCH (J-SL ST): Insert hook from WS to RS through sl st on lower circle, then insert hook from RS to WS through sl st on upper circle, yarn over, draw yarn through both sl sts and lp on hook.

+ PATTERN NOTES +

- Acrylic version of rug is worked with 2 strands of same color yarn held together throughout.
- Use a nonslip pad under the rug if placed on a wood floor, tile, or any other smooth surface.

RUG

CIRCLE MOTIF

Make 60 (45 MC, 8 CC, and 7 CC1).

RND 1: (RS) With MC, CC, or CC1 and smaller (9 mm) hook, make an adjustable ring, (see sidebar on page 130), 8 sc in ring, pull tail end tight to close ring, sl st in 1st sc to join. *Note:* Secure the yarn end by weaving it in with yarn needle before clipping it close to the work.

RND 2: Ch 1, 2 sc in each sc around, sl st in first sc to join—16 sc.

RND 3: Ch 1, 2 sc in 1st sc, sc in next sc, * 2 sc in next sc, sc in next sc, rep from * around, sl st in first sc to join, place a st marker in sl st just made—24 sc.

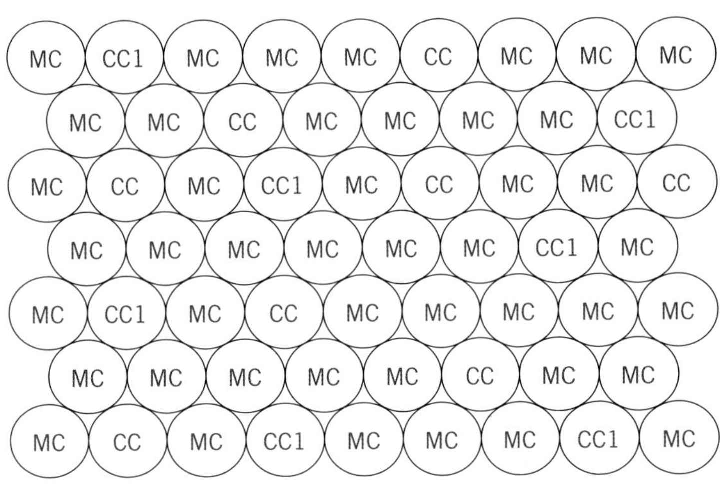

figure 1. Circle motif and color arrangement.

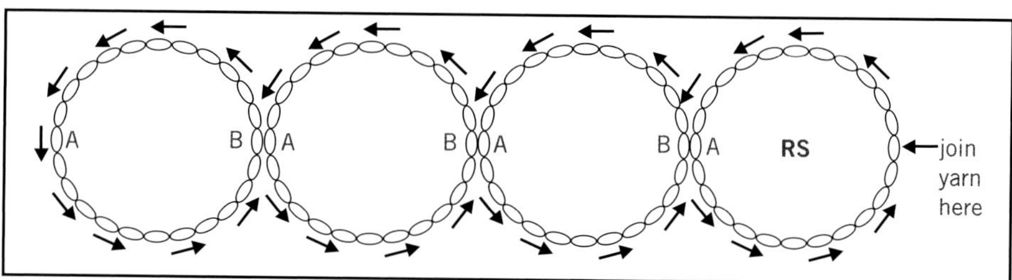

figure 2. Joining circles into rows. Diagram shows fewer circles than are actually in a row. Ovals represent sl sts of Circle Motif Round 4.

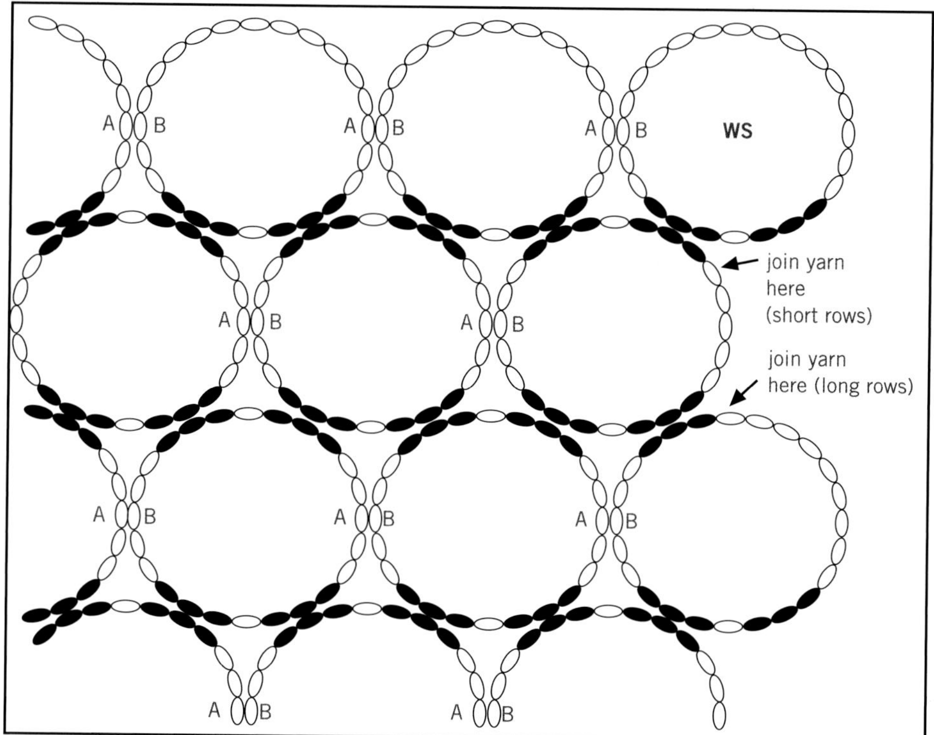

figure 3. Joining rows. Ovals represent sl sts of Circle Motif Round 4. Dark ovals indicate stitch pairs to be joined together.

RND 4: Sl st loosely in blo of each sc around and in blo of marked sl st from previous round (remove marker) (24 sl st). Fasten off, leaving a long tail end, about 10" (25.5 cm). Do not weave in this end because it will be used during rug assembly.

FINISHING

ARRANGE CIRCLES

Lay out all circles, with RS facing, according to Figure 1 or your own color arrangement. *Tip:* If you are creating your own color arrangement, take a photo of your rug now (or draw a quick sketch of color placement), in case your project is moved before assembly is complete.

JOIN CIRCLES INTO ROWS

Each row of circles will be connected by crocheting a sl st border around them. Stitch A and Stitch B (Figure 2) will each contain 2 sl sts after border is complete. By joining the circles at a specific stitch, the circles become positioned so that the tail end of each circle is close to where it is joined to the next circle. Sew with this tail to give additional strength to the connection point between circles. Circles should lie flat after bordering; if they cup, the sl sts are too tight. *Optional:* Use a larger hook, size N or P/15 (10 mm), to keep sl sts loose and even.

First Circle: With yarn CC2, 9 mm or 10 mm hook, and RS facing, join yarn in 12th sl st before tail end on first circle (Figure 2), sl st loosely in next 11 sl st, flip tail end of circle over working end of yarn to keep tail end neatly out of the way, sl st loosely in next sl st (Stitch A, Figure 2).****Next Circle:*** Bringing the next circle (RS facing) very close to st just made, make a snug sl st in 12th sl st before tail end of circle, sl st loosely in next 11 sl st, flip tail end of circle over working end of yarn to keep tail end neatly out of the way, sl st loosely in next sl st (Stitch B, Figure 2); repeat from * to end of row. Continuing with the last circle in row, sl st loosely in next 11 sl st and Stitch B. *****Next Circle:*** Make a snug sl st in st in Stitch A, sl st loosely in next 11 sl st and Stitch B; repeat from ** to end of row. Sl st in first sl st where yarn was joined. Fasten off. When weaving in each circle tail end that lies between two circles, sew discreetly back and forth a few times at the point where two circles are joined and then weave in the end as usual.

JOIN ROWS

To keep rows in order during assembly, label them before turning them WS facing for assembly, as follows: On small pieces of masking tape, write each row number and next to it draw an arrow pointing upwards. Stick the corresponding label on the back of the end circle of each row, with arrow pointing towards top of rug. Labeling rows is not necessary if a single color is used for all circles.

Turn all rows over so that WS is facing. Work into sl sts of Circle Motif Round 4, not sl sts of row border. You may wish to mark stitches according to Figure 3 or count stitches as you join. Begin by joining Row 2 to Row 1, then join Row 3 to Row 2, and so on. Instructions are written for joining a short row (Rows 2, 4, 6) to a long row; changes for joining a long row (Rows 3, 5, 7) to a short row are given in brackets.

*****Joining a short (long) row:*** With smaller hook, MC, and WS facing, join yarn in sl st indicated (Figure 3), *j-sl st (see Special Stitches) loosely in next sl st pair indicated (Figure 3) 3 times, sl st in next sl st of lower (upper) circle, j-sl st loosely in next sl st pair indicated (Figure 3) 3 times, sl st in next sl st of upper (lower) circle; repeat from * to end of row. Fasten off. Repeat from ** until all rows are joined. Weave in ends with yarn needle.

technically speaking: THE ADJUSTABLE RING

One of the most popular articles on CrochetMe.com is Donna's tutorial on *The Magic Adjustable Ring*, a way to crochet in the round without the pesky hole in the middle of your work. Adding this simple technique to your arsenal will make you feel like a crochet superhero.

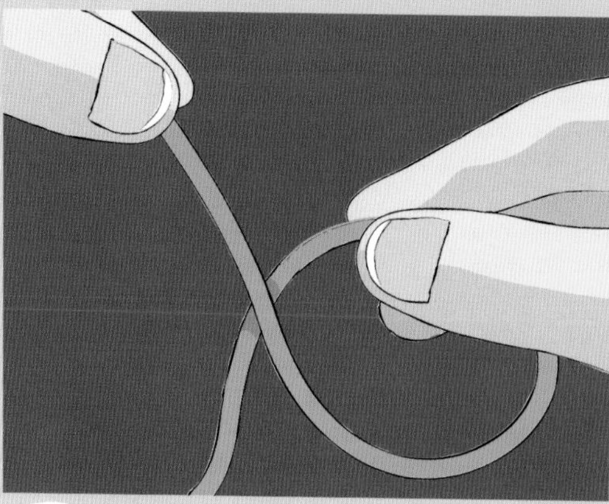

1 Leaving a 6" (15 cm) tail, make a ring by placing the tail end of yarn behind the working yarn.

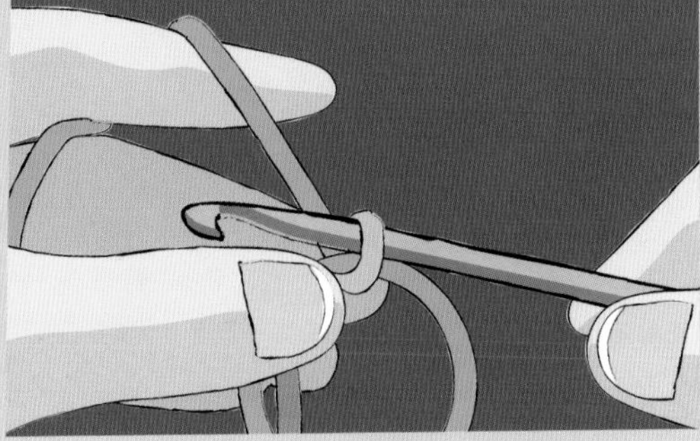

2 Insert your hook from front to back through the center of the ring, yo with the working yarn, and pull up a lp. Ch 1 (this assumes you'll be making sc sts. Ch the appropriate number if you'll be making hdc, dc, etc.).

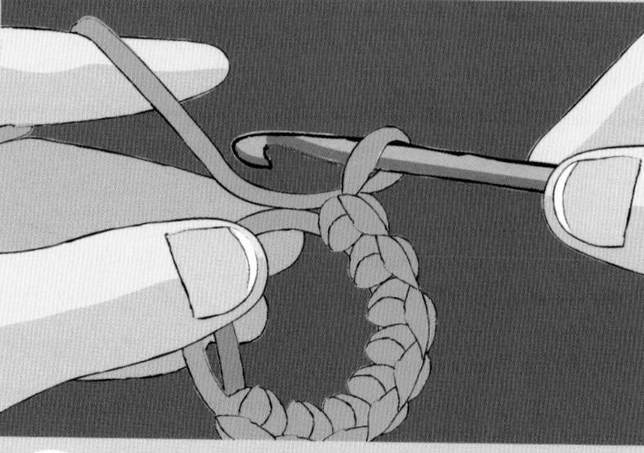

3 Continuing to hold the ring closed with your nondominant hand, work several sc sts into the ring, covering the tail.

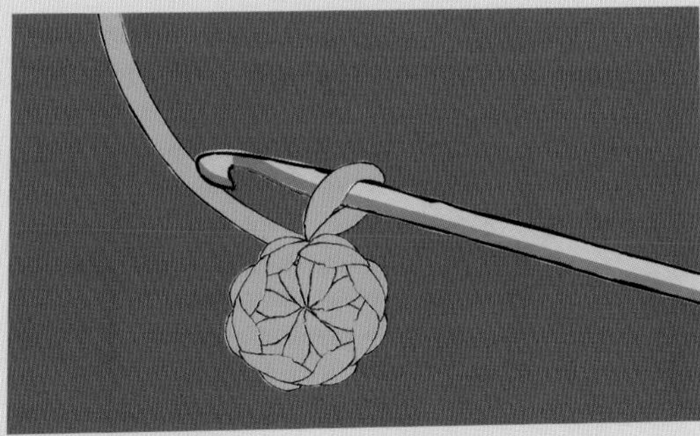

4 Pull the yarn tail to tighten the ring. Presto! No hole in the center of your work. Continue to work in the round as usual.

designer in profile

donna hulka

PHOTO BY BRYAN H. HULKA.

Zeitgeist is a word that gets tossed around a lot in design communities and on the Web in a sort of watered-down way common with buzz terminology. It refers to lots of people thinking about or doing a similar thing at the same time. In March 2004 as I was experiencing the magic of the Internet for the first time and CrochetMe.com was just getting off the ground, the Crochetville.org message board was just starting out, too. And a woman named Donna started a blog called Yarn Tomato. Here's how she puts it: "My site started as a crochet blog, mostly for myself. I didn't expect much more than the occasional visitor. I never imagined it would lead to discovering an immense world of crocheters, becoming a crochet designer, having my patterns published in books, and appearing on TV. Yarn Tomato now also includes free patterns and tutorials and my design portfolio." The time was right.

I liked Donna immediately for her thoughtful, measured, and otherwise even-keeled manner. Donna became one of the moderators of the Crochetville.org community that as of this writing exceeds 10,000 members. She's written some of the most popular tutorials and patterns in CrochetMe.com and has remained a close and trusted friend. She has often kept me company when she couldn't sleep on the East Coast and I was up late on the West Coast putting together an issue of the magazine.

Donna has a background in natural resources, forestry, and soils. She grew up with a big, wooded backyard where she used to make soda-bottle terrariums. She now enjoys, "a quiet life in eastern North Carolina with my husband, son, and golden retriever. I love dogs, tomatoes, blue crabs, being at home, the smell of rain on concrete. I'm a perfectionist. I'm an avid recycler. I keep things too long and when I part with them, I like to make sure they go where they will be needed, loved or at least useful. I love the slip stitch and what it can do, so you'll see it often in my work."

SAY HELLO TO DONNA AT YARNTOMATO.COM.

ED

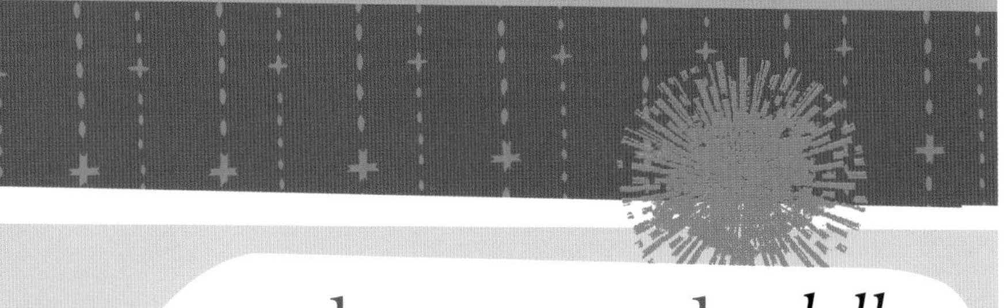

doug + gordo *dolls*

Kim Werker

concentration rating 1 **2** 3 4

KIM'S INSPIRATION

I have a short attention span, which is why my favorite things to crochet are scarves and dolls. I can finish them up before I get bored and start thinking about the next thing I want to make. For the book, I wanted to jack things up a little and make big dolls. One is the loneliest number, so I had to make two. Also, I'm an American expat living in Canada and continue to be enamored with all things stereotypically Canadian. So these dolls are Canucks, through and through. Gordo and Doug like curling, peameal, hockey, poutine, and—to the dismay of hosers—grits. With a luxe exoskeleton of bulky yarn crocheted on a small hook, these guys are terrific for cuddling or for just hanging around looking good.

FINISHED SIZE

13" (33 cm) high and 7" (18 cm) diameter at the base.

YARN

Lion Brand Yarns Wool-Ease Thick & Quick (80% acrylic, 20% wool; 106 yd [97 m]/170 g). *Gordo (blue):* #106 sky blue (MC), #99 fisherman (CC1), #112 raspberry (CC2), 1 ball each. *Doug (green):* #132 lemongrass (MC), #99 fisherman (CC1), #133 pumpkin (CC2), 1 ball each.

SUBSTITUTION: About 100 yd (91 m) bulky-weight (Super Bulky #6) yarn for MC and small amounts of bulky-weight yarn for contrast colors.

HOOK

Size L/11 (8 mm) and size D/3 (3.25 mm) (optional). Change hook size if necessary to obtain correct gauge.

NOTIONS

Yarn needle; eyes; sewing needle; 1 yd (1 m) sewing thread; contrast yarn/thread for facial features; polyfill stuffing, 1 bag for each doll; 5 yd (5 m) size 10 white crochet thread (optional) for eyes.

GAUGE

10 sc and 10 rows = 4" (10 cm) with larger hook .

Gauge is not critical in this pattern, but make sure your stitches are tight so the stuffing doesn't bleed through.

+ PATTERN NOTES +

- All work in the round is done in a spiral, so do not join stitches at the end of each round. Place a marker in the last stitch of the round. When you reach the marker remove it, work the stitch(es), and replace it to mark the last stitch of the round.

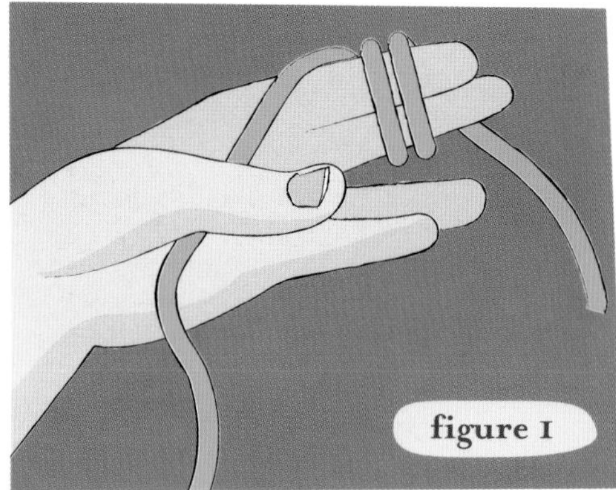

figure 1

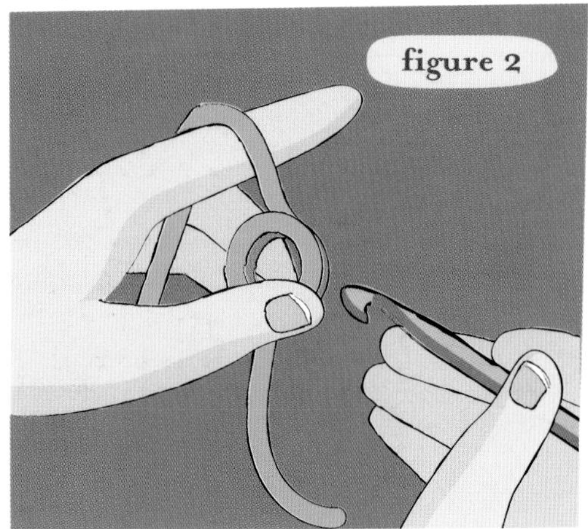

figure 2

HEAD

With MC, wrap yarn twice around the first two fingers of your nondominant hand, leaving a 2" (5 cm) tail (Figure 1). Remove the ring from your fingers, keeping hold of the tail to keep the ring intact. Insert larger hook through the center of the ring and pull up a lp (Figure 2). Ch 1.

RND 1: Work 6 sc into the ring. Pm in last sc to mark the end of the round. Pull tail end to tighten ring—6 sc.

RND 2: Work 2 sc in each st around—12 sc.

RND 3: *Sc in next st, 2 sc in next st; rep from * around—18 sc.

RND 4: *Sc in each of next 2 sts, 2 sc in next st; rep from * around—24 sc.

RND 5: *Sc in each of next 3 sts, 2 sc in next st; rep from * around—30 sc.

RND 6: *Sc in each of next 4 sts, 2 sc in next st; rep from * around—36 sc.

RNDS 7–8: Sc in each st around.

RND 9: *Sc in each of next 5 sts, 2 sc in next st; rep from * around—42 sc.

RNDS 10–18: Sc in each st around.

RND 19: *Sc2tog over next 2 sts, sc in each of next 5 sts; rep from * around—36 sc total.

Sl st in next st. Fasten off, leaving a 24" (61 cm) tail.

BODY

With MC, begin with a double ring as for Head, ch 1.

RND 1: Work 8 sc into the ring. Pm in last sc to mark the end of the round. Pull tail end to tighten ring—8 sc.

RND 2: Work 2 sc in each st around—16 sc.

RND 3: *Sc in next st, 2 sc in next st; rep from * around—24 sc.

RND 4: *Sc in each of next 2 sts, 2 sc in next st; rep from * around—32 sc.

RND 5: *Sc in each of next 3 sts, 2 sc in next st; rep from * around—40 sc.

RND 6: *Sc in each of next 4 sts, 2 sc in next st; rep from * around—48 sc.

RND 7: *Sc in each of next 5 sts, 2 sc in next st; rep from * around—56 sc.

RND 8: Start shaping the pot belly. Sc in each of next 25 sts, (work 2 sc in next st) twice, sc in each of next 2 sts, (work 2 sc in next st) twice, sc in each st to end of round—60 sc.

RND 9: Sc in each st around.

RND 10: Sc in each of next 25 sts, *work 2 sc in next st, sc in next st, work 2 sc in next st*, sc in each of next 4 sts, rep from * once, sc to end of round—64 sc.

RND 11: Sc in each of next 5 sts, sc2tog over next 2 sts, sc in each st to 7 sts before end of round, sc2tog over next 2 sts, sc in each of next 5 sts—62 sc.

RND 12: *Sc2tog over next 2 sts, sc in each of next 5 sts, [sc2tog over next 2 sts, sc in each of next 6 sts] 3 times; rep from * once—54 sc.

RND 13: *Sc2tog over next 2 sts, sc in each of next 7 sts; rep from * around—48 sc total.

RNDS 14–15: Sc in each st around.

RND 16: Sc in each of next 18 sts, sc2tog over next 2 sts, sc in each of next 8 sts, sc2tog over next 2 sts, sc in each st to end of round—46 sc.

RND 17: Sc in each st around.

RND 18: Sc in each of next 19 sc, [sc2tog over next 2 sts] 4 times, sc in each st to end of round—42 sc.

RND 19: *Sc2tog over next 2 sts, sc in each of next 5 sts; rep from * around—36 sc.

RND 20: Sc in each st around.

RND 21: Sc in each of next 13 sts, hdc in each of next 10 sts, sc in each st to end of round. Sl st in next st. Fasten off.

ARMS

Work the arms in the following stripe patterns. Always change color by working the last st of the round until 2 lps remain on the hook, complete the st with the new yarn. Because the inside of the arm will be hidden from view, don't cut the yarn if the color will be used again. Simply drop it and pick it up when it's needed again.

STRIPE PATTERN 1—GORDO (BLUE)

ROWS 1-2: CC1.

ROWS 3–7: CC2.

ROW 8: MC.

ROWS 9–11: CC2.

ROWS 12–13: MC.

ROWS 14–15: CC2.

ROWS 16–18: MC.

ROW 19: CC2.

ROWS 20–24: MC.

STRIPE PATTERN II—DOUG (GREEN)

ROWS 1–2: CC1.

ROWS 3–8: MC.

ROWS 9–21: CC2.

ROWS 22–24: MC.

Begin with a double ring as for Head, ch 1.

RND 1: Work 6 sc into the ring. Pm in last sc to mark the end of the round. Pull tail end to tighten ring—6 sc.

RND 2: Work 2 sc in each st around—12 sc.

RND 3: *Sc in each of next 2 sts, 2 sc in next st; rep from * around—16 sc.

RND 4: Sc in each st around.

RND 5: *Sc2tog over next 2 sts; rep from * around—8 sc.

Stuff the hand just enough so that you're still comfortable working the next round of stitches.

RNDS 6–24: Sc in each st around. Sl st in next st. Fasten off, leaving a 10" (25.5 cm) tail.

EYE BACKINGS

(Make 2, optional)

With size 10 crochet thread and smaller hook, begin with a double ring as for Head, ch 1.

RND 1: Work 8 sc into the ring. Pm in last sc to mark the end of the round. Pull tail end to tighten ring—8 sc.

RND 2: Work 2 sc in each st around—16 sc.

RND 3: *Sc in next st, 2 sc in next st; rep from * around—24 sc.

Fasten off, leaving an 8" (20.5 cm) tail.

FINISHING

If you're using eyes that having a fastener on them, attach them to the head or backing before stuffing. Stuff the head and body; do not stuff the arms beyond the hands (this allows them to be nice and flexible). When you think you're done stuffing, stuff some more. The head and body use almost an entire bag of stuffing. With yarn needle and long tail from head, line up the sl st from the head and body and whipstitch them together. Using the tail ends, sew the arms to the neck area. If you're not using eyes with a fastener, sew eyes to the head. Using yarn or thread, embroider the mouth and any other facial features. If you're so inclined, crochet your happy Canadians a toque. Or hair. Or, you know, ears.

Note that small parts are not baby- or toddler-friendly. If you're willing to part with your doll by putting it into the hands of a being who will drool on it, make sure you use only embroidery and no embellishments that can be swallowed. The same goes for older children who might be inclined to shove small parts up their nose or in their ear. And for grown-ups who are, um, immature.

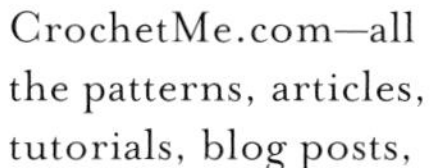

postscript

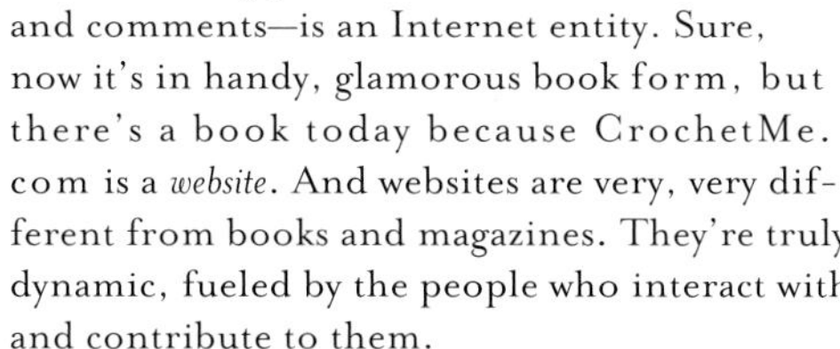

CrochetMe.com—all the patterns, articles, tutorials, blog posts, and comments—is an Internet entity. Sure, now it's in handy, glamorous book form, but there's a book today because CrochetMe.com is a *website*. And websites are very, very different from books and magazines. They're truly dynamic, fueled by the people who interact with and contribute to them.

The initial success of CrochetMe.com came about because a lot of people were looking for fresh resources for crochet inspiration. They blogged about the website, posted on message boards about it, and told their friends about it. The continued success of the site came about because people were generous with their ideas, creativity, time, and energy.

If you're reading this, you should be a member of CrochetMe.com. You're obviously interested in crochet and in exploring your creativity. Put this book down now and fire up your Web browser. Here is an annotated list of websites I find particularly fabulous or at least helpful for crochet information, design ideas, and more:

CROCHET

CrochetMe.com—Go. Now.

InterweaveCrochet.com—A treasure trove of content. Again, I'm biased.

Crochetville.org—Über-welcoming crochet community.

CrochetPatternCentral.com—A massive directory of links to free crochet patterns.

Crochet.org—Official website of the Crochet Guild of America.

Ravelry.com—Organize your yarn life!

YarnStandards.com—This site, created by the Craft Yarn Council of America, lists standard crochet abbreviations, offers a U.S./metric hook size conversion chart, and gives standard garment and hat sizes for babies, children, and adults.

CRAFT AND DESIGN

Craftster.org—Thousands and thousands of very creative, crafty people sharing tips, tricks, reviews, patterns, and all sorts of crafty conversation.

Craftzine.com—For all the latest and wackiest crafts online.

DesignSponge.com—All design (mostly for the home), all the time.

Flickr.com—Free photo sharing/social networking site. There are loads of crafty groups on this site—the potential for inspiration is endless. Also, this site is a great tool for bloggers.

WhipUp.net—A collaborative blog about crafts of all sorts.

WEBSITES OF THE DESIGNERS FEATURED IN THIS BOOK

Robyn Chachula: crochetbyfaye.com

Megan Granholm: loopdedoo.blogspot.com

Missa Hills: midnightknitter.com, kpixie.com

Julie Holetz: skamama.com

Amy O'Neill Houck: aohdesigns.com, hookandi.blogspot.com

Donna Hulka: yarntomato.com, crochetville.org

Cecily Keim: suchsweethands.com

Chloe Nightingale: galvanic.co.uk

Kristin Omdahl: styledbykristin.com

Annette Petavy: annettepetavy.com

Carol Ventura: tapestrycrochet.com

abbreviations

BEG	begin(s); beginning
BET	between
BLO	back loop only
CC	contrasting color
CH	chain
CM	centimeter(s)
CONT	continue(s); continuing
DC	double crochet
DEC(S)('D) DECREASE(S);	decreasing; decreased
EST	established
FDC	foundation double crochet
FSC	foundation single crochet
FLO	front loop only
FOLL	follows; following
G	gram(s)
HDC	half double crochet
INC(S)('D) INCREASE(S);	increasing; increased
LP(S)	loop(s)
MC	main color
M	marker
MM	millimeter(s)
PATT(S)	pattern(s)
PM	place marker
REM	remain(s); remaining
REP	repeat; repeating
REV SC	reverse single crochet
RND(S)	round(s)
RS	right side
SC	single crochet
SK	skip
SL	slip
SL ST	slip(ped) stitch
SP(S)	space(es)
ST(S)	stitch(es)
TCH	turning chain
TOG	together
TR	treble crochet
WS	wrong side
YD	yard
YO	yarn over hook
*	repeat starting point
* *	repeat all instructions between asterisks
( )	alternate measurements and/or instructions
[ ]	work bracketed instructions a specified number of times

STANDARD YARN WEIGHT SYSTEM

Yarn Weight Symbol And Category Names	1 SUPER FINE	2 FINE	3 LIGHT	4 MEDIUM	5 BULKY	6 SUPER BULKY
Type of Yarns in Category	Sock, Fingering, Baby	Sport, Baby	DK, Light Worsted	Worsted, Afghan, Aran	Chunky, Craft, Rug	Bulky, Roving
Crochet Gauge* Ranges In Single Crochet To 4 Inches	21–32 sts	16–20 sts	12–17 sts	11–14 sts	8–11 sts	5–9 sts
Recommended Hook in Metric Size Range	2.25–3.5mm	3.5–4.5mm	4.5–5.5mm	5.5–6.5mm	6.5–9mm	9mm and larger
Recommended Hook in U.S. Size Range	B-1 to E-4	E-4 to 7	7 to I-9	I-9 to K-10½	K-10½ to M-13	M-13 and larger

* GUIDELINES ONLY: The above reflect the most commonly used gauges and needle or hook sizes for specific yarn categories

glossary

CROCHET CHAIN (CH)

Make a slipknot on hook. Yarn over hook and draw it through loop of slipknot. Repeat, drawing yarn through the last loop formed.

SINGLE CROCHET (SC)

Insert hook into a stitch, yarn over hook and draw a loop through stitch (Figure 1), yarn over hook and draw it through both loops on hook (Figure 2).

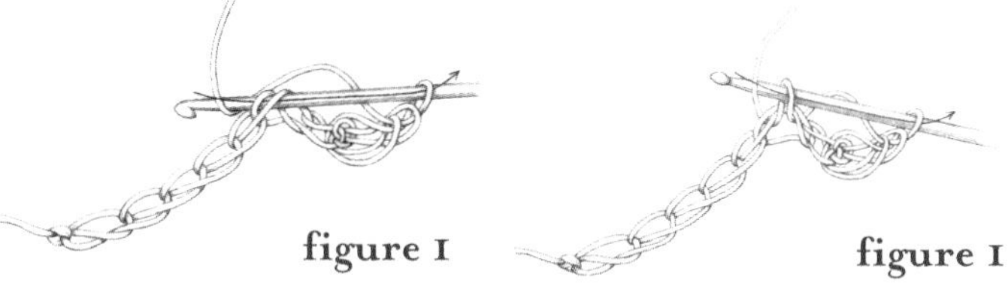

figure 1 figure 1

Foundation Double Crochet

Step 1: Yarn over, insert hook in 3rd chain from hook, yarn over and draw up a loop (3 loops on hook), yarn over and pull through 1 loop (1 chain made), [yarn over and pull through 2 loops] 2 times—1 edc; the beginning of a row of foundation double crochet (Figure 1).

Step 2: Yarn over, insert hook under the 2 loops of the chain you made in the first edc in Step 1 (Figure 2), yarn over and draw up a loop (3 loops on hook), yarn over and pull through 1 loop (1 chain made), yarn over and pull through 2 loops, yarn over and pull through 2 loops (Figure 3)—1 foundation double crochet st.

Step 3: Yarn over, insert hook under the 2 loops of the chain you made in the foundation double crochet st in Step 2 (Figure 4), yarn over and draw up a loop (3 loops on hook), yarn over and pull through 1 loop (1 chain made), [yarn over and pull through 2 loops] 2 times. Rep Step 3 as needed (Figure 5).

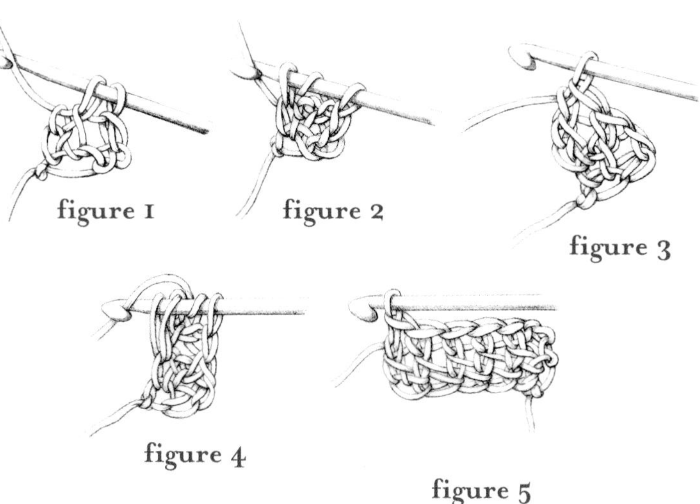

figure 1 figure 2 figure 3 figure 4 figure 5

SINGLE CROCHET 2 TOGETHER (SC2TOG)

Insert hook in next stitch, yarn over, draw loop through stitch (2 loops on hook, Figure 1). Insert hook in next stitch, yarn over, draw loop through stitch (3 loops on hook). Yarn over and draw yarn through all 3 loops on hook (Figure 2). Completed sc2tog—1 stitch decreased (Figure 3).

figure 1

figure 2

figure 3

HALF DOUBLE CROCHET (HDC)

*Yarn over hook, insert hook into a stitch, yarn over hook and draw a loop through stitch (3 loops on hook), yarn over hook (Figure 1) and draw it through all the loops on the hook (Figure 2). Repeat from *.

figure 1

figure 2

DOUBLE CROCHET (DC)

*Yarn over hook, insert hook into a stitch, yarn over hook and draw a loop through stitch (3 loops on hook; Figure 1), yarn over hook and draw it through 2 loops (Figure 2), yarn over hook and draw it through the remaining 2 loops (Figure 3). Repeat from *.

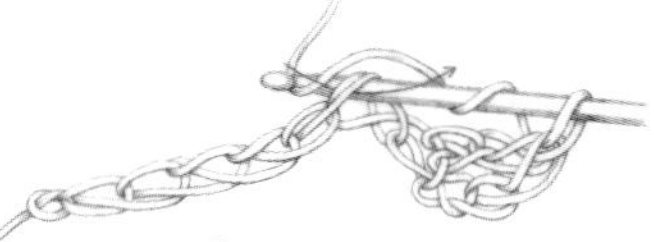

figure 1

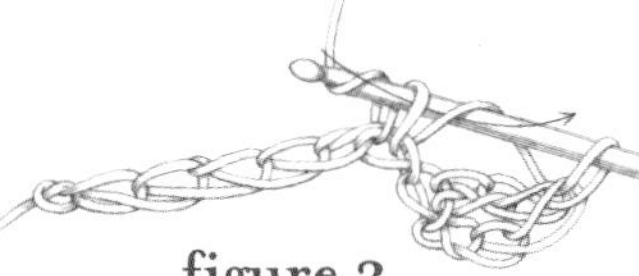

figure 2

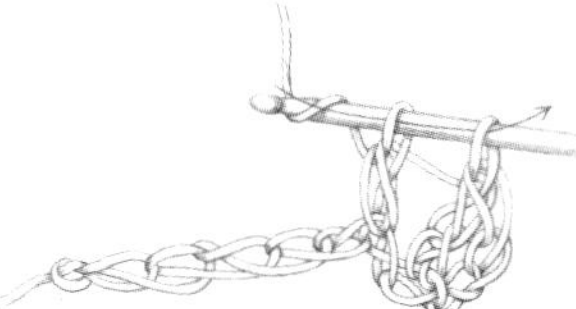

figure 3